The Future
of the
American Past

by Earl H. Brill

a study course
on American values

A CROSSROAD BOOK

THE SEABURY PRESS · NEW YORK

The Seabury Press
815 Second Avenue
New York, N.Y. 10017

LIBRARY OF CONGRESS CATALOGING IN PUBLICATION DATA

Brill, Earl H
   The future of the American past.

   "A Crossroad book."
   1. United States—Religion.   2. United States—Civilization. I. Title.
BR515.B74   209'.73   73-17890
ISBN 0-8164-2086-6

Contents

Introduction

This generation of Americans has known affluence and well-being. We have also witnessed social upheaval, protest, and dissent. We have seen our cities in flames, violence and disorder in our streets. Some of our most gifted leaders have been struck down by assassins; unarmed students have been shot down by National Guardsmen and police. Our institutions of government have been brought into disrepute by the manipulations and chicanery of some of our highest officials. It is with a sense of urgency, not of idle speculation, that we ask each other, "Where is America going?"

This nation, we have been accustomed to believe, was founded on democratic principles tested throughout nearly two hundred years of historical experience. The bicentennial anniversary of the signing of our Declaration of Independence is a time to stop and reflect upon the present status of these traditional values.

The religious community bears a particular responsibility for this kind of self-evaluation. As people dedicated to justice, liberty, truth, and love, we need to go beyond the popular celebrations, the commercial extravaganzas, the tourist specials that are features of our commemoration of the bicentennial. We are inheritors of the prophetic tradition that seeks to discover God's will for the present time, what God would have us do in our situation.

The bicentennial can be a God-given opportunity for us to reflect, not only on our past, but on our future. What are the significant themes and values of our historical tradition? How do they fare today? How do we stand with respect to them? What do they imply for our future?

This book is intended to help contemporary American Christians raise and discuss such questions as these. They come out of a process of reflection and discussion involving theologians, secular scholars, and dedicated lay men and women. In July 1973,

The Anglican Theological Review published a special issue called *A Creative Recovery of American Tradition* which consisted of essays by nine scholars of varying backgrounds who sought to identify some of the major issues arising out of the American experience. In an introductory essay, the editor, W. Taylor Stevenson, listed as unifying themes the relationship of religion and culture, the motif of pilgrimage, and the witness to the experience of mystery. Those threads of our heritage have been employed as the central categories of this analysis. To them have been added the concept of mission, which looms large in our history, and the complementary/contradictory values of freedom and equality, without which no discussion of the American tradition would be coherent. Readers who wish to pursue these issues further should turn to the special issue of *The Anglican Theological Review* for guidance. (See page 81 for their address.)

This book is not intended to be a summary of American religious history. Dealing with some (not all) of the major themes and values of our national life, I have tried to show how they are each a product of our religious heritage, but I have been concerned as much with their secular meanings and impact as with their religious dimension. Though the Christian community can be expected to play a significant role in the American future, whatever values we bring to that future are likely to be shared by many who do not regard themselves as Christians.

In developing the various issues under discussion, I have felt free to introduce my own opinions whenever they have seemed appropriate, but at the same time I have tried to respect the reader's freedom to make up his or her own mind. We are considering important aspects of our everyday lives, affecting how we feel about our country, about each other, and about ourselves. We are apt to have strong views about such questions, and sometimes our views will conflict with the equally strong views of others.

The purpose of this study course is to shed some light on our basic values, to get them out into the open, to think about them, to talk about them, and to relate them to the decisions we make

about our lives. Not every Christian will come out on the same
side of every issue, nor should we expect that to happen. The
best we can hope for is that our opinions will be based on sincere
and thoughtful reflection rather than on mere prejudice. Where
our views are colored by self-interest (and most of them are),
we owe it to the lord of truth (and to ourselves) to acknowledge
it. Where our views conflict, we owe it to each other to try to
understand opposing viewpoints, to learn from them, and to
respect the right of others to hold them. If we can study and
reflect with this attitude, we may not find agreement, but we
may go a long way toward building a base of understanding and
mutual trust, which is not a bad foundation for moving into the
future.

Session plans are included for use when the book is employed
in an educational program. Although it has been designed primarily for use by discussion groups, the book itself can be read,
hopefully for profit and pleasure, by people who do not take part
in a course. It has been written for that elusive audience: average,
educated lay men and women. While numbers of serious scholarly books are available to us, the works that can bring the
products of that scholarship to the general public are still in short
supply. I hope this book may help to fill that need.

Because the book is intended for the nonspecialist, I have
omitted the customary scholarly apparatus of footnotes, but there
is a short list of suggested readings after each chapter.

ACKNOWLEDGMENTS

I would like to express my thanks to the Reverend James C.
Fenhagen for the help he gave in the design of the six study sessions. I am particularly grateful to the group of lay men and
women of St. Columba's Church in Washington, D.C., who tested
the design with me and offered many valuable criticisms. Char-
lotte Fletcher, also of St. Columba's, deserves special thanks for
her expeditious typing of the manuscript.

EARL H. BRILL

Advent 1973, Washington, D.C.

I

Christian and American:

THE INTERPENETRATION OF RELIGION AND CULTURE

The United States Supreme Court has declared that "We are a religious people whose institutions presuppose a Supreme Being." That may be putting the matter a little too strongly, but religion *has* played a very significant role in shaping American culture and has been shaped by it in return.

Religious faith is always experienced and lived out in the context of culture, the particular social environment in which the religious person lives. Culture shapes our perceptions of reality and provides us with language, beliefs, values, attitudes, and customs. Even when our convictions change, the changes themselves are influenced by our culture.

No Christian has ever been just a Christian and nothing more. He may be a Christian and a farmer, a Christian and a businessman, a Christian and a Roman citizen. A Christian may be also an American, a schoolteacher, a lover of the outdoors, a Republican, a property owner, a husband and father—or wife and mother—and a football fan.

Every life includes a multitude of commitments: religious, professional, political, social, aesthetic, recreational, etc. A person's religion is lived out in the midst of these other commitments, some of which support religion and some of which conflict with it.

The relation of religious commitments to political commitments has been a problem for Christians since the time of the New Testament. The issue was raised when Jesus was asked whether it was lawful to pay taxes to Caesar. It was raised again when gentile Christians in the early church sought to be freed from Jewish dietary restrictions. St. Paul was letting a cultural standard determine Christian practice when he decreed that women should keep their heads covered in church.

There is no one definitive answer to these religion/culture questions in the New Testament. Jesus answered by stating that we owe something to Caesar and something to God. If that means that we have some obligations to public authority and some obligations to God, what are we to do when the two authorities conflict? And how do we know when we are truly serving God and when we are serving the nation, society, culture. As we examine our American heritage, how are we to sort out what has its roots in Christianity and what comes from some other source?

The Relationship of Religion and Culture

Down through history, the Christian community has offered a variety of answers, based on widely different assessments of culture and different concepts of how Christians should relate to the world they live in. Some years ago, in a book entitled *Christ and Culture*, H. Richard Niebuhr analyzed some of the ways in which sectors of the Christian community dealt with their culture in the past. He described five kinds of relationships between Christ and culture:

Christ against culture
Christ of culture
Christ above culture
Christ and culture in paradox
Christ transforming culture

These categories may help us understand ways in which we relate our American values to our religious heritage.

Christ Against Culture

This view is based on the belief that culture, "the world," is under the rule of Satan. In the Fourth Gospel, Jesus himself refers to Satan as "the prince of this world." In the Book of Revelation (chapter 18), the Roman state is depicted as the great whore of Babylon, polluting the earth. That is not too surprising, since Rome was actively persecuting the Christians at the time.

The "Christ against culture" perspective demands that the committed Christian abandon or oppose the secular order. "Choose ye whom ye shall serve!" is its motto. It may call for a radical dissociation from society and the erection of a separate social system, as has been the case with the Amish in America. It may call for a stand against symbolic identification with the society, as when Jehovah's Witnesses refuse to salute the American flag. It may involve militant opposition to the whole social system, as when Daniel Berrigan observes that the only respectable place for a committed Christian in America today is in jail.

Christ of Culture

This view stands at the opposite pole from the "Christ against culture" view. It takes the culture as its starting point and tries to fit religion into cultural categories. It sees no basic conflict between religion and culture. Where there seems to be conflict, religion must be redefined or reinterpreted so that it can make sense to men of the culture.

Modern theologians who want to reinterpret the Gospel so that it can be accepted in the scientific age have adopted the "Christ of culture" view. So have those who identify Christianity with the American way of life or with the free enterprise system. When Western missionaries moved into Asia and Africa during the nineteenth century, they brought not only the Gospel but also the products of Western culture. They fought polygamy, put blouses on the bare bosoms of native women, proclaimed human equality, established schools, and founded hospitals. These activities, worthy as they may seem, represented nineteenth-century Western European and American expressions of Christianity. Such missionaries were proclaiming the Christ of their culture.

Christ Above Culture

The medieval church regarded civilization as fundamentally good because it is part of God's creation, yet incomplete in itself. Reason, in this view, needs to be fulfilled by revelation; knowledge by faith; the philosophical virtues of courage, temperance, and wisdom by the theological virtues of faith, hope, and charity. Theology is queen of the sciences, while the Church is *mater et magister*, mother and teacher, of the society.

This viewpoint is associated with medieval Catholicism, but it is very much alive in America today, in both Catholic and Protestant circles. When American Protestants crusaded for the prohibition of liquor, they were asserting the superiority of Christ over culture. So was the National Council of Churches when it called on the government to recognize Communist China. Ministers who mount the pulpit to tell statesmen how they ought to perform their duties may not be asserting the impressive power of the medieval popes, but they are assuming, just as the popes did, that Christ reigns over culture.

Christ and Culture in Paradox

This position is characterized by contradiction, paradox, tension, and ambiguity. It is not easy to explain. Yet it has a long and impressive pedigree in Christendom, going back as far as St. Paul, who accepted the existing social order but at the same time saw it under the judgment of God. Martin Luther held a similar view and believed, further, that human sinfulness penetrates into the highest spiritual realm.

According to this view, culture makes legitimate claims upon us, just as Christ does. Our obligations as citizens are as valid as our obligations as churchmen. At the same time, both culture and religion stand under judgment because of sin. Because he is a sinner, man can do no good thing, either culturally or religiously. Only God's grace and forgiveness enable him to stand as justified sinner. He can act in the world only because he knows that God forgives him.

On its positive side, this viewpoint enables people to participate fully in the ambiguous world of political and economic life. Reinhold Niebuhr's political realism was deeply informed by this paradoxical view of Christ and culture. But this dynamic view has some built-in booby traps. For example, if you are convinced that because of sin, no one can do anything good, then you may find it easy to justify your own participation in evil since evil is inevitable.

If the conflicting claims of religion and culture make you anxious, you may ease the tension by simply separating the "spiritual" realm from the "secular." The church can reign supreme in its sphere while the civil order goes unchallenged in its sphere. The separation of church and state in America has frequently led to this result. As Tocqueville remarked more than a century ago, "In America religion is a distinct sphere, in which the priest is sovereign, but out of which he takes care never to go."

Christ Transforming Culture

This perspective, like the "Christ above culture" view, is based on the belief that society is fundamentally good because it was created by God. But the transformist also believes that civilization stands under God's judgment because of the failures and imperfections that result from human sinfulness. He sees Christ's work as the redemption of the fallen world and the church's work as the transformation of culture into the kingdom of Christ.

The transformist may not be an unqualified optimist, but he believes that patient and persistent effort can bring about orderly change in the society. He is essentially a reformer, a gradualist, seeking to eliminate injustice and exploitation. Since he is convinced that Christ works in all people, not only in conscious believers, he has no trouble in cooperating with secular movements in order to bring about those changes in the society that he regards as consistent with the mind of Christ.

In America this view was widely shared by the leaders of the nineteenth-century social gospel movement as they sought to bring the rule of Christ to modern industrial society. The political reformers of the progressive era were their secular allies. In our own time, civil rights activists have drawn on the "Christ transforming culture" viewpoint, as have many religious leaders of the peace movement.

Religion and the American Past

In our analysis of American culture, it will become clear that religion has had much to do with making us what we are as a people. Many of our common values, attitudes, ideas, and assumptions have come from our religious tradition and are maintained even by those who have repudiated the religious heritage itself. Our belief in the sanctity of personal life, our humaneness, our sense of destiny, our belief in the moral law that transcends the laws on the books—all these are products of our religious past.

But our religion has bequeathed some less attractive qualities as well: our tendency toward officious moralizing, for example, and our compulsive commitment to work. We have an unfortunate habit of treating with contempt anyone who does not have a job. We have, on the whole, a rather high opinion of ourselves. And we have to acknowledge that aspects of our religious heritage have been used to justify some of these unattractive characteristics.

While religion has helped to shape American society, positively as well as negatively, the American environment has done much to shape our religious life. The separation of church and state, which most of the established churches originally opposed, has given us a religious atmosphere different from anything known in Christendom until modern times. In America the churches are voluntary societies, which the members support by their free-will offerings. Laymen exert enormous influence in our churches. There is a wide range of religious alternatives in our society, and little religious conflict. Our churches are highly organized and active, but show little interest in sustained theological reflection.

Church members, like other Americans, are optimistic, prag-
matic, and individualistic. It is this peculiarly American character of our religion, rather than the religious character of America,
that most impresses foreign visitors.

Our heritage in church and nation is, to be honest, a mixture
of both good and evil, strength and weakness, achievement and
failure. How can responsible Christians best relate themselves to
that past? That is a difficult question for any morally sensitive
American who knows something about his past and for whom
a simple-minded, uncritical patriotism is inadequate.

There have been great achievements in our past. We should
neither deny nor minimize them. We can be justly proud of them,
as we are proud when someone we know does some great deed
or wins some great honor. But we cannot take any credit for
those accomplishments. We were not on the scene when independence was won. We did not frame the Constitution, or free
the slaves, or tame the continent. We are the beneficiaries of
those achievements. We can only accept the benefits with joy
and gratitude—and with perhaps a little awe and reverence
mixed in.

The evils in our past are harder to deal with. What can we
say about slavery, the slaughter of the Indians, the terrible economic exploitation, the violence against the immigrant, the corruption, racism, anti-Semitism? These things are part of our past,
too. We cannot leave them out when we evaluate our culture.

I believe that we have every reason to feel deeply ashamed of
these elements in our history, just as we are ashamed of the
skeletons in our family closet. If your great-grandfather was a
manufacturer who grossly underpaid his workers and fired them
if they voted the wrong way on election day, then you probably
don't brag very much about him. If you mention him at all, it is
likely to be with a certain sense of shame and regret.

Shame and regret, to be sure, but not guilt. After all, you don't
have to feel guilty about your great-grandfather. You don't have
to take the blame for him. His sins are not your sins. Of course, if
he left you his fortune, you might well try conscientiously to

compensate the victims of his exploitation. But you don't have to bear the burden of his sins. You have sins of your own to bear.

We could say the same about the sins of our national history. We ought to deplore the slave trade, but we don't have to feel guilty about it. We weren't involved in it, and we don't have to take any blame for it. We can feel ashamed of the soldiers who murdered the Indians at Wounded Knee, but we weren't there. We did not participate in or approve of the killing. Consequently we don't have to feel any guilt about it. Since we did inherit the Indians' land and the results of slave labor, we do have an obligation to try to redress those wrongs in our time.

I make this point at some length because we Americans find it difficult to come to terms with this mixture of good and evil in our history. Many people would prefer to forget about the evil, the failures, the errors of the past; to act as though they never existed. They are embarrassed when they hear that Lincoln was a conniving politician, that Washington was a poor administrator, that Jefferson was both, so they would rather not mention such matters. They want to minimize the conflict, the violence, the injustice and exploitation so prominent in the American past.

On the other hand, many thoughtful and sensitive Americans become so angry and disillusioned when they first confront the evils in our past that from then on they refuse to believe anything good about the country. They feel a sense of outrage when they learn what was done to the Indians, the Negroes, the immigrants, and other exploited groups. They come to regard the nation as thoroughly corrupt and decadent, its values not even worth discussing.

Both these attitudes are distorted and unproductive. If we avoid the negative aspects of our history, we wind up being naïve and self-righteous. We can make no significant contribution to the future because we have never faced the whole truth about the past. But at the same time, we do have to begin by affirming the culture. If we do not basically love our country and have some faith in its future, there is no point in making discriminating criticism of it. For we criticize our past so that we can better understand what we need to do to shape our future.

In the pages that follow, I have tried to hold affirmation and criticism in balance. There is much in our national life that cries out for change. But behind the criticism lies the conviction that while America is by no means perfect, we have in our heritage much that is worth preserving. The American tradition, properly understood and interpreted, can still furnish us with a solid foundation for a worthwhile future.

SUGGESTED READINGS

H. Richard Niebuhr, *Christ and Culture* (New York: Harper, 1951) sets forth the religion/culture analysis used in this chapter. Sydney E. Ahlstrom, *A Religious History of the American People* (New Haven: Yale University Press, 1972) is the most complete account of the subject. Alexis de Tocqueville's nineteenth-century classic *Democracy in America*, 2 vols. (New York: Vintage Books, 1945) contains much insight into the religious aspect of American culture. Winthrop Hudson, *The Great Tradition of the American Churches* (New York: Harper & Row, 1963) emphasizes the spirit of independence and self-direction in American Protestantism. Sidney E. Mead, *The Lively Experiment* (New York: Harper & Row, 1965) is a perceptive set of essays on religion in the American environment.

II
On Pilgrimage:

THE AMERICAN QUEST

Remember how you used to celebrate Thanksgiving when you were in elementary school? People would dress up like Pilgrims, with black coats and tall black hats, and would act out that first Thanksgiving, when the original Pilgrims of Plymouth Plantation sat down with their Indian friends to give thanks for their survival through the first hard year of colonial life.

Those Pilgrims occupy an important place in our national memory. Not only do they offer us inspiration because of what they accomplished, but they also furnish us with one of our significant national symbols: the pilgrimage, the quest, the journey to tomorrow.

A pilgrim is a traveler, but a peculiar sort of traveler. He is defined by the character of his destination: he is on his way to a holy place. He may enjoy the trip, as the pilgrims did in Chaucer's *Canterbury Tales.* He may encounter hardships along the way, as Pilgrim did in Bunyan's great allegory. But at the end of the trail, real benefits await him, spiritual benefits: healing, ecstasy, answers to prayers, association with the relics of saints and martyrs.

The small band of settlers who landed at Plymouth in 1620 defined themselves as Pilgrims, wanderers on the face of the earth, in search of a land where they could act out their religious convictions and order their church life free from the meddling and harassment of English civil authorities. At the same time, they wanted to preserve their heritage as Englishmen, which they had been afraid of losing during their stay in Holland. God, they believed, had called them to this quest for a homeland.

Likening themselves to Israel in the wilderness, they saw in this new "promised land" the opportunity to build Zion in New England.

Many groups of settlers who came to America during the seventeenth and eighteenth centuries considered themselves on a pilgrimage. Historians disagree on whether the colonists came here for religious freedom or for economic advancement. Both motives played a part, no doubt, in some cases one more than the other. In recent years economic interpretations of history have tended to write off religious motivations as mere rationalizations. But this viewpoint does not do justice to the importance of religious concerns for most people in those centuries.

The New England Puritans would have been the first to concede that their great migration was a commercial venture; that is what their charter provided. But at the same time, and more important to them, it was an effort to build a biblical commonwealth, a New Israel, where the Puritan version of Christian faith could be established and lived out. They did not, of course, harbor any sentimental notions about tolerance or religious freedom. They had a view of what the Good Society should be, and they were determined to bring it into actuality.

During those early years, other religious dissenters were led to make a similar voyage to the New World. Quakers came to escape persecution in England, and William Penn launched his Holy Experiment as a place of refuge, not only for his own religious associates, but for all persecuted peoples. German Pietists, such as the pacifist Moravians, came to avoid compulsory military service. The theme of pilgrimage looms large in the colonizing process during those years. It is reflected in the place names the settlers chose when they build towns: Salem, Bethel, Nazareth, Bethlehem.

The Changing Meaning of the Quest

As time went on, the intensity of religious conviction waned, and the pursuit of economic opportunity escalated. Maybe this was because the longed-for religious freedom soon became an actual fact. No need for a pilgrimage to seek a goal already achieved. Or maybe the increasing prosperity of the eighteenth century seduced the pilgrims from their original goal. Affluence, it seems, is a greater peril to spiritual growth than is persecution.

The change has been noted by every historian who has dealt with the period. It is neatly summed up in the oft-repeated phrase about the Friends who "came to do good and did well instead." The Puritan was being transmuted into the Yankee: the sharp trader, the shrewd, tightfisted merchant, builder of fortunes, a founder of lines of Boston blue bloods.

In the course of American history, then, the pilgrimage has remained a significant symbol, but its meaning has been drastically altered. What was once a spiritual quest has become a commercial quest. The end sought for has been, not the kingdom of God, but the kingdom of Mammon.

It is not unfair to say that most of the later immigrants were driven by economic rather than by religious motives. Not that they were lured by greed; they were driven by want and necessity. In nineteenth-century Europe, famine, overpopulation, and industrialization forced peasants off the land and into the cities, where there were often no jobs for them. To such people, America could easily be seen as a land of opportunity: the opportunity to work, to earn enough to support a family, perhaps even to own land, to become self-sufficient, to rise in the world. Such aims are not contemptible even though they may seem modest.

Meanwhile, those already in America were moving to the frontier, founding new towns and cities, developing mines, building factories, railroads, clipper ships—all in a quest for increased prosperity. Boosterism ran wild. Speculation made and unmade fortunes. Credit was tight, expanded, collapsed. By the end of the nineteenth century, we were in the midst of "the great barbecue," and everybody wanted some.

As the nature of the quest changed, there was a corresponding change in the terminology used to interpret it. We heard less of the biblical commonwealth and New Jerusalem. The myth was now couched in economic terms: "Rags to riches"; or in political terms: "Log cabin to White House." The American dream was born, a dream of material prosperity, physical comfort, wealth and possessions.

A People on the Move

This active, energetic, and persistent pursuit of economic advancement has had a profound effect on the American character, on our behavior, our life style, our way of relating to each other. It has produced a population that is constantly on the move. Throughout the nineteenth century, immigrants poured into the Eastern cities, farmers moved west, while others moved from farm to city, in search of better opportunities.

In our own time, geographical mobility has become second nature. In *A Nation of Strangers*, Vance Packard has recently pointed out that we are the most mobile people in the world. The average family moves every five or six years. Most of us have relatives and friends scattered all over the nation. Even if we stay put, it seems that everyone around us is always moving away.

As a result, we have become a restless people. If you don't move, you feel that you should. In the white-collar world, a man knows he is doing a good job only when someone offers him a better one. Fifteen years on the same job is an evidence of failure. To move up the promotion ladder, you have to be prepared to move wherever you are called. Whether in business, government, the military, the university, or the church, the same standard applies.

People in motion relate to other people in particular ways. Americans are noted for their capacity to move easily into new situations, to make new friends rapidly, to adjust to new conditions resourcefully. That's no surprise, since we spend much of our lives practicing these skills. But on the other hand, we often lack the capacity for intimacy and depth in our interpersonal relations. And many people will tell you frankly that since they know in advance that sooner or later, relationships with their friends will have to be broken off as one of them moves away, it doesn't pay to become too deeply involved with other people. Parting is only that much harder to take when you do.

Whatever its cost in personal terms, the quest for economic well-being has paid off in its own coin. By 1950 the United States could boast of having achieved the highest standard of living of any nation in the history of the world. That phrase, "standard of living," deserves analysis because it says far more about us than we intend. For what is a standard? It is a norm, a yardstick by which we measure the value of things. The standard of life might conceivably refer to an index of virtue, or justice, or righteousness. But for us, the phrase has meant the level at which we consume economic goods and services. How much do you spend? What do you buy? What do you own? The phrase makes it clear that we have adopted an economic interpretation of the meaning and value of our lives.

What happens to a pilgrim when he reaches his destination? Healing perhaps, or enlightenment, or fulfillment. Or even possibly salvation. Or it may be that the promised land looks less promising once you've arrived there.

This seems to be what has happened to these United States. It is no accident that the late 1950s saw the launching of a debate about our "national purpose." The major magazine carried extended articles on the subject. Commentators and social critics argued about what it was, what it should be. A presidential commission was appointed to consider the matter. The question became important precisely at the moment in our history when we entered the age of our greatest affluence. It illustrates the observation that the poor man finds it easy to believe that all his problems would be solved if only he had money. The wealthy—individual or nation—is denied that illusion. In the age of affluence, the pilgrim path peters out in a wasteland of consumer goods that fail to produce satisfaction, or security, or even much fun.

In making this point, I do not mean to suggest that we should downgrade prosperity or feel guilty because we have it. I certainly would not want to give up the stereo set and LP records that enable me to retreat into the baroque era whenever I am fed up with the present. Prosperity, like happiness, is a good by-product of a journey that leads somewhere. It is not a satisfactory destination in itself.

When prosperity becomes the pilgrim's destination, it subjects every thing, every person, every value to the tyranny of the profit motive. Everything in life is given a dollar value. When acquisitiveness engages us in an insatiable pursuit of profits and goods beyond what we can reasonably use, it has become an evil. That kind of striving can destroy personal life, family life, friendship, serenity. It is also responsible for the exploitation of the poor and powerless, the corruption of government, the plunder of the continent, and the deterioration of our cities.

Resuming the Pilgrimage

There are faint signs that America is becoming disillusioned with affluence and that the climate is being created for a renewal of the spirit of pilgrimage. In recent years, among the young there has been what looks like a massive defection from the pursuit of the once almighty dollar. Students drop out of college to travel and explore the world and themselves. Young professionals reject the pressures of the rat race to experiment with alternative life styles: new forms of family life, schools, work environments, and communities. Exploration of inner space has led some into experiments with drugs, meditation, encounter groups, and other kinds of "humanistic psychology." The vast and amorphous human-potential movement has already begun to institutionalize some of these experiments in reflection and interaction. Many of these innovations will turn out to be dead ends, of course, but the climate of experimentation is more important than the particular forms in which it is expressed.

More and more responsible middle-class Americans are finding ways to assert in their own lives their concern for a quality that goes beyond what we used to call our standard of living. We all know men of genuine competence and talent who have turned down impressive jobs with large salaries in order to remain in the community where they have come to feel at home, or in order to have adequate time to spend with their families. This may seem quite contradictory to the pilgrim's readiness to strike out for new territory, but perhaps a choice not to accept a promotion which flies in the face of the ordinary expectations of our society may be a very innovative decision. To stay put may be the most novel decision a man ever makes.

Such developments may mark the beginning of a new awakening of our sense of spiritual pilgrimage—secular though its forms may seem. Once again, men and women are asking what makes life significant and are taking whatever steps lie in their power to seek the answer. I don't believe that all this ferment represents merely a lusting for psychological kicks—an emotional quest by the man who has everything. Of course it contains elements of pleasure seeking, titillation, faddism. But mixed in with all that's kooky is some of that pilgrim vision, the yearning for significant experience in the realm of the spirit.

Such a quest needs to be balanced by a concern for society. People who cultivate the inner self cannot afford to lose sight of God's demand for social justice, righteousness, and compassion for the poor and the powerless. If the spiritual quest serves only as a hiding place for the weak and timid who fear the stresses of political and social action, it will be destructive.

Those who have lost the vision of the Good Society are the enemies of the pilgrimage. The early Puritan fathers castigated those who were too much "at ease in Sion," who enjoyed their own prosperity and cared for little else. Prosperity can be an enemy if it leads to complacency, to feeling "I've got it made." The comfortable and the complacent are the fat "cows of Bashan" against whom Amos prophesied.

Some have lost the vision because they are too comfortable. Others have lost it because they are too fearful. Like the Israelites who wanted Moses to take them back to Egypt, they would abandon the pilgrimage and retreat into the past—usually a past that never was. Embalming the customs of other ages, they cling to a version of the past that justifies their own values and interests.

The Old West of novels, movies, and TV shows is a case in point. Pop culture glamorizes the lawlessness of the period of settlement, makes heroes out of vicious killers, celebrates the practice of "taking the law into your own hands," treats the Indian and Mexican (especially the sinister "half-breed") with undisguised contempt. As entertainment, this may be harmless, but in terms of meaning and values, it distorts our view of the past and teaches precisely the wrong lessons for the present.

Disneyland or Frontier Town—or even Colonial Williamsburg —may delight the eye and provide wholesome family entertainment, but these artificial environments shed very little light on the quality of American life in other times. As you wander through Williamsburg's quaint colonial buildings, so carefully reconstructed with Mr. Rockefeller's millions, you wonder why anyone would ever want to leave such a lovely town. There is no sign of the thick mud that could trap a carriage between Mr. Wythe's mansion and the State House, or of the mosquitoes that brought the yellow fever that finally caused the colonial government to abandon the place. And there is little evidence of the institution of slavery that made it all possible.

We can restore the buildings, reenact the festivities, and reintroduce the crafts of an earlier day, but we cannot restore the customs, reenact the events, or reintroduce the values—nor would we want to if we could, at least not if we fully understood them. Those who would live in the past can neither resurrect the past nor deal adequately with the present. Antiquarianism and nostalgia may serve some as temporary defenses against the storms of the present, but they are not the equipment of the pilgrim.

Those seventeenth-century Pilgrims who settled in America did indeed maintain a lively sense of the past. They read widely in ancient literatures: the Bible, the Greek and Roman philosophers, statesmen, poets, and dramatists. They learned their les-

sons from history—but they did not take refuge in it. They were
thoroughly knowledgeable about their own time and place. They
were well aware of the novelty of their effort. They set out quite
consciously to do a new thing.

In a curious sense, we are in a similar position. We have accumulated more of a past to be aware of, but we are still in
transition, as they were. America is still something of an experiment, and we are still not sure whether it will succeed or fail.
But the idea, once thought revolutionary, that the common people can be trusted to govern themselves has become so widespread that it is accepted even where it is denied in practice.

Nevertheless, our situation is still unique in many ways. According to economists, we are the first nation to enter the stage
of high mass consumption. We have pushed the uses of advanced
technology further than any other society. We have developed
mass communication to a level never before seen in the world.
We are in the midst of trying, in the words of the Prayer Book,
to "fashion into one united people the multitudes brought hither
out of many kindreds and tongues." We are trying to produce
genuine equality in this diverse society, while affirming the particularities of various races, sexes, and ethnic groups. All these
developments are taking place under the aegis of a popularly
elected government.

No nation has been this route before. Every major decision in
public policy, every significant social change is an innovation.
In other words, we are still pioneers; America is still the trail-
blazing society. For us modern pioneers, the frontier seems less
exotic, less attractive, less exciting. It consists of crowded cities,
hectic suburbs, huge faceless institutions. It is as easy to get lost
in these spaces as in the wilds of the territory that Lewis and
Clark explored.

Can we make this new wilderness our home? It is not entirely
clear yet. The pilgrim would say: "By God, let's try." For the
pilgrim, we are in transit to a destination prepared by God, a
holy city, a new society. The pilgrim is under no illusion that he
has arrived. He knows that the journey may be long and difficult;

that he may never live to see its ending. He knows that he may have to travel light, that some things he holds dear may have to be laid aside along the way. But God calls him to the journey, and he responds by moving on.

There is an old bromide that patriotic speakers often used to close their speeches on the Fourth of July: "Hats off to the past. Coats off to the future." It's corny, but it sums up the pilgrim attitude precisely. The pilgrim affirms his history. He accepts it without complaint, with gratitude for its benefits, and a sense of humility and compassion toward its shortcomings. But the future is still open. We have an opportunity to make it what we will. The pilgrim cheerfully accepts that responsibility and sets to work in the conviction that he can play some small part in the building of the future.

SUGGESTED READINGS

Frederick Tolles, *Meeting House and Counting House* (Chapel Hill: University of North Carolina Press, 1948) discusses the interaction of religious and commercial values in the Quakers of eighteenth-century Philadelphia. Irvin G. Wyllie, *The Self-Made Man in America* (New York: The Free Press, 1966) explores the rags-to-riches myth as it relates to the realities of our business civilization. Moses Rischin, ed., *The American Gospel of Success* (Chicago: Quadrangle Books, 1965) is a collection of readings on the subject from Cotton Mather to John Kenneth Galbraith, with a perceptive introduction in which the editor traces the idea of success back to its roots in the religious tradition. Kenneth Lynn, *The Dream of Success* (Boston: Little, Brown, 1955) analyzes the literary response to the idea of success in such writers as Theodore Dreiser, Jack London, and Frank Norris. Vance Packard, *A Nation of Strangers* (New York: McKay, 1972) ponders the effect of sustained and rapid mobility on the American character. For a relatively optimistic view of the emerging challenge to acquisitive values in America, see Theodore A. Roszak, *The Making of a Counter-Culture* (Garden City, N.Y.: Doubleday, 1969).

III

The Mission of America

In his influential book *The Course of American Democratic Thought*, first published in 1940, the historian Ralph Gabriel stressed the idea of "the Mission of America" as one of the basic themes of the American democratic faith. Americans believe their country has a mission in the world. Whether that has been a good thing or a bad thing for the world is a matter of debate.

"Mission" and "pilgrimage" may sound like different words for the same idea. And in fact, the pilgrim journey may be seen as a mission, an attempt to move into a new future. On the other hand, the pilgrim and the missionary may be seen as opposites— the missionary attempting to shape the world while the pilgrim tries to leave it behind.

In the American tradition, I think the missionary and pilgrim themes complement each other. The New England Pilgrims and the Puritans, who followed them, were consciously on pilgrimage. But at the same time, they were just as consciously engaging in a mission for which they believed that God had chosen them. When they called their colony a city set upon a hill, they were referring directly to Jesus' injunction in his Sermon on the Mount:

> You are the light of the world. A city that is set on a hill cannot be hidden, nor do men light a candle and put it under a basket, but on a candlestick, so that it gives light to the whole house. Let your light so shine before men that they may see your good works and glorify your father who is in heaven.
>
> (Matt. 5:14–16)

The meaning of that passage is clear. The Lord's faithful are to live in such a way that others may see the goodness of their lives and be led to praise the God whom they serve. It implies that those who see will be led to imitate what they see. Jesus' disciples are to be God's demonstration project; they are to create a model of community, with justice and righteousness, for all the world to see and imitate.

That is just what the New England settlers had in mind. They had given up on the Old World, but the New World offered new possibilities. In coming to America, they were, in a sense, running away from the past, but they were also moving toward a new future, a future in which God's rule on earth would be made manifest for all the world to see. They intended to bring about the rule of the saints, and they had no doubt that saintly men in other lands would learn from their experience.

A more conventional concept of missionary work was in the minds of those settlers and other early colonists as well. In both New England and Virginia, the spread of the Gospel and the conversion of the Indians was stated as one of the reasons for the original colonizing expeditions. Historians sometimes regard these pronouncements as pious window dressing, but there is no reason to doubt their sincerity, even though these efforts bore little fruit.

Not only did the mission to the Indians fail, but in a significant sense, the biblical commonwealth failed as well. The unanimity between the clergy and the magistrates that had made Massachusetts a theocracy soon broke down. Though preachers would lament the decline of religious fervor, and revivalists would later try to reawaken it, discord, dissent, and dissonance would be the hallmarks of New England's religious life.

The Revolution as Mission

Political issues began to replace religious issues as the leading topics of controversy in colonial America after the middle of the eighteenth century. Lawyers and the clergy of nearly all the churches—except for some Anglicans—argued for the God-given rights of freeborn Englishmen, including even the right to revolt against a king who had transgressed the limits that God had set for a monarch. When the American Revolution was launched, it met widespread support from Christian ministers.

The leaders of the Revolution saw in their actions an example for the rest of the world. In the minds of men such as Jefferson, Madison, and Adams, the new nation was embarking on an experiment to determine whether ordinary men could govern themselves without falling into either mob rule or oppression. Conventional political wisdom said they could not. In Europe the simple folk followed monarchs and nobles because they were as convinced as their leaders that some men were born to rule, others to be ruled.

Those American democratic republicans who won the Revolution and framed the government for the new nation hoped that their success would inspire others to imitate them. They expected that their strike for independence would touch off a wave of revolutions throughout Europe, that crowned heads would fall, and that a new era of republican government would begin in which all men would be free.

It was not an idle hope, as the history of the next half-century was to demonstrate. Fifty years after the Declaration of Independence, Jefferson, writing only a few weeks before his death, expressed the meaning of the Declaration for all mankind:

May it be to the world, what I believe it will be . . . the signal of arousing men to burst the chains under which monkish ignorance and superstition had persuaded them to bind themselves, and to assume the blessings and security of self-government. . . . All eyes are opened, or opening, to the rights of man. The general spread of the light of science has already laid open to every view the palpable truth, that the mass of mankind has not been born with saddles on their backs, nor a favored few booted and spurred, ready to ride them legitimately, by the grace of God. These are grounds of hope for others.

America, in the eyes of Jefferson and his colleagues, still had a mission. It was to be the laboratory of democracy, a demonstration, not of God's kingdom, but of man's ability to rule himself. America was to offer the example that would encourage the common people everywhere.

The Churches' "Mission to America"

Mission in a more ecclesiastical sense emerged as an important theme as the nineteenth century began. The nation seemed to be at a low ebb of religious vitality and commitment. The gradual separation of Church and state which followed the revolution had changed the role of religion in society. In 1880 a small percentage of the total population could be listed as active church members. Moreover, as settlers moved westward, they tended to lose contact with the institutions of traditional religion, education, and culture.

It was in this climate, feeling both their own weakness and the great opportunities that lay before them, that the churches mobilized what can only be termed a "mission to America." It was directed against atheism, backsliding, and Romanism. The term they used was "home missions." Denominational, interdenominational, and nondenominational agencies were founded to support missionaries; distribute Bibles, tracts, and books; found schools and colleges—all in the attempt to bring Christianity and civilization to people regarded as only slightly removed from barbarism. Winning the West for Christ was a working out of the "Christ transforming culture" concept.

Along with the mission to the frontier went a movement back home for moral reform and regeneration. Experimental communities were one part of this movement. Relief for the poor and prison reform was another part. Some churches launched ministries to the urban worker, the aged, the orphan, the sick. But the largest and, ultimately, the most significant expressions of the movement were the efforts for temperance and the abolition of slavery.

A mission will inevitably be evaluated on the basis of where you sit with respect to it; whether you are missioner or missionee. Martin Marty has referred to this mission to America as a "Righteous Empire," hinting that it consisted primarily of a tendency toward coercive morality. The ingredient of self-righteous meddling is there, to be sure. But a mission is almost always the result of some people's vision of the good life. Since they know it to be good, they want to share it. When they see what they regard as injustice or immorality, they try to change it. But if they are out to condemn and change you, you may very well regard them as officious meddlers. The evils the churches fought during this period of American history, however, were real ones. Slavery particularly was offensive on both Christian and political grounds.

We should take special note of a virulent anti-Catholic strain in this mission to America. For the white Protestant American was apt to be as anti-Catholic as he was to be racist. Anti-Catholicism was his unreflective response to the feeling of being surrounded by a powerful and dangerous foe. Militant Catholicism was staging a return to power on the European continent. In France especially, it was outspokenly reactionary, antidemocratic, and aggressive. No wonder the American Protestants were convinced that the newly arrived foreigners were out to build a Catholic power in the United States.

This does not justify the anti-Catholic rhetoric, the Know-Nothing politics, the mob violence directed against Catholics, the discrimination against the Irish in employment, or the more subtle forms of bigotry common at the time. But the presence of a perceived threat to American and Protestant institutions helps to explain the persistence of the anti-Catholic theme in the Protestant missionary movement.

Any missionary movement may be seen as aggressive and self-righteous by those who are its objects. This was certainly true of Southerners in their response to the antislavery crusade. They saw the abolition movement as unwarranted interference in their internal affairs by New Englanders who themselves were no better than they should be. The New Englanders decried the sinfulness of slavery, they pointed out, but treated their own wage workers even worse than slaveholders treated their slaves. New England, they claimed, was out to destroy the genteel, leisurely plantation system in order to build a nation of money-grubbing shopkeepers. And as for the Free-Soilers of the Middle West, they opposed slavery, not out of moral compassion for the Negro, but out of fear of his competition.

The slavery question was settled, belatedly and tragically, by the Civil War, which was seen in missionary terms by both North and South. Indeed, the war may have been prolonged and intensified by the moral fervor of the preachers on both sides. But the nation did come together again to find a new unity on the basis of a political version of American mission. From the beginning, this aspect had been developing alongside the more explicitly religious missionary movement.

Now political mission won the support of both political parties for a drive to expand the borders of the United States to encompass the entire continent. It was seen as our "manifest destiny" to occupy the land "from sea to shining sea," and many would have liked to incorporate Canada and Mexico into the republic, as well.

Manifest destiny was a journalist's phrase, but the idea behind it was illustrated by wagons moving westward, by voyages around Cape Horn to search for gold in California, by war with Mexico, and almost by a war with Canada. By the end of the nineteenth century, America's political mission was successful. Her manifest destiny had been fulfilled.

The Mission to the World

The restless, energetic, and now powerful nation saw the world as its sphere of action. Long before this time, Protestant missionaries had discovered China, not to mention Japan, Latin America, and Africa. Merchants too had covered the globe, sailing into ports on every continent. The successful conclusion of

the Spanish-American War served notice on the world that the
United States had arrived.

From now on, the American mission would be stated in global
terms. President William McKinley, recounting how after prayer
and meditation he had come to the conclusion that the United
States should annex the Philippines, put the matter into the perspective of Christian responsibility:

> There was nothing left for us to do but to take them all and
> to educate the Filipinos and uplift and civilize and Chris-
> tianize them and by God's grace do the very best we could
> by them, as our fellow men for whom Christ also died.

Enthusiastic global thinkers developed a grand rationale for
America's role in world affairs. It was based on a view of the
superiority of the Anglo-Saxon "racial stock." They explained
that Anglo-Saxons had given the world the highest form of government, republicanism, and the highest form of religion, Protestant Christianity. It was the duty of these peculiarly fitted
people to spread the advantages of both republican government
and Protestant Christianity to those lesser breeds that did not
enjoy the benefits of either.

The more hard-nosed version of this doctrine asserted that the
Anglo-Saxons had been schooled for the final competition of
races, which in God's providence they were sure to win. Josiah
Strong, clergyman, publicist, and general secretary of the pan-
Protestant Evangelical Alliance, is often quoted as an archetypal
representative of this viewpoint:

> Then this race of unequalled energy, with all the majesty
> of numbers and the might of wealth behind it—the repre-
> sentative, let us hope, of the largest liberty, the purest
> Christianity, the highest civilization—having developed
> peculiarly aggressive traits calculated to impress its insti-
> tutions upon mankind, will spread itself over the earth.

And can anyone doubt that the result of this competition of races will be the survival of the fittest.

The American mission, in other words, was to bring civilization, Christianity, and democracy to the rest of the world—by force, if necessary.

But it was idealism as much as imperialism or self-interest that propelled the nation into world politics. While it is true that political and economic concerns lay behind our entry into the First World War, nevertheless the mass of Americans responded to the argument that the purpose of the war was to make the world "safe for democracy." It was genuinely perceived to be a "war to end all wars," and it was on that basis that preachers uncritically urged their congregations to greater exertions in the war effort.

Postwar disillusionment matched wartime idealism, as it always does, and Americans turned away from international involvements during the period of the "twenty years' crisis" from 1919 to 1939. But war came upon us again, whether we liked it or not. It is fair to say however that the patriotic fervor of World War II did not reach the jingoistic excesses of the earlier war. The fact that the new war began with an enemy attack made it possible to justify our entry in strictly defensive terms. And it took no great propaganda effort to picture the nazi power as the demonic power of darkness. Hitler saw to it that the realities of his regime far outstripped the worst that enemy propagandists could say about him.

Yet a sense of mission did pervade the war effort. The "free world," or "the United Nations," was contrasted with "the slave world" of totalitarianism in U.S. Government rhetoric. The war was interpreted as an effort to eliminate slavery and dictatorship. The alliance with Stalin's Russia constituted only a small embarrassment, since Russia was obviously fighting a defensive war for survival. It is quite in the spirit of the American mission concept that General Eisenhower entitled his account of the campaigns on the western front *Crusade in Europe*. Only Americans, at this late date in history, still mounted crusades.

Following the close of World War II, the United States engaged in a decade-long debate about the merits, the perils, and the shape of internationalism. Isolationism was out of fashion, but proponents of that doctrine still held important positions in the Congress and in the economic establishment. But in time, they too made the shift, and internationalism became an unchallenged cornerstone of American foreign policy.

The concept of mission entered into this discussion and may well have provided the victory for the internationalists. The key to the American mission in the postwar years was anticommunism. The cold war was its central focus. Missionary terminology was commonly applied to the international struggle, for example, the frequently repeated phrase "winning the hearts and minds of men"—a political type of conversion experience.

America's sense of mission manifested itself in two ways. In the first place, the nation saw itself as the undisputed leader of the free (noncommunist) world. It was the linchpin in a set of interlocking alliances from Western Europe to Southeast Asia. It was the source of economic and military assistance to all the nations within that sphere. Its announced purpose was to halt the spread of communism in the world. This purpose also had a religious dimension: the defense of Christian civilization against the forces of Godless communism. Private agencies sprang up to aid the cause, with names such as The Christian Anti-Communist Crusade.

In support of this mission, the United States established military bases all over the world. Thousands of troops and civilians, naval vessels, and airplanes were stationed from the Mediterranean to the Far East. The nation responded regularly to crises on every continent. In doing so, the United States was motivated, please note, not primarily by a quest for power or wealth, as its critics often claimed. These interventions were understood as acts of international responsibility carried out on behalf of other people, in the interest of peace and freedom.

In the second place, the United States saw itself as a model for the newly emerging nations, which clearly looked to this country for leadership and inspiration. At the end of World War II we were asking ourselves, "Is American democracy exportable? If not, what is there in our way of life that other countries can make use of?"

The answer seemed to be not our Constitution, our two-party system, or even the "free enterprise" system itself. The newly developing nations appeared far more impressed with our high standard of living and our economic abundance than with our individual freedom or our institutional arrangements. "How can we enjoy what you now have?" they seemed to ask.

Economic development was to be the answer. American economists and policymakers set out to develop schemes to enable pre-industrial societies to move into the industrial age. They soon decided that political stability was necessary before economic development was feasible. So, while we invested both public and private funds in industrial development, we embarked on a policy of supporting existing noncommunist governments to provide political stability. Thus we set about to train policemen and armed forces. We exported arms at discount rates until our military-assistance program rivaled our expenditures for economic assistance. The long-term result was that for the first time in its history the United States came to be regarded throughout the world as a counterrevolutionary power.

This twin policy—the crusade against communism and the program of economic and military assistance to developing nations—came together in Vietnam, resulting in America's most tragic disaster in the twentieth century. It produced the most controversial war in our history, deeply divided the nation, and touched off a debate on our role in the world that is not yet over.

I don't propose to carry on that debate here; I merely want to record the fact that it is still with us. Many Americans continue to believe that the Vietnam venture was a legitimate exercise of international responsibility, the defense of a free people. The opposition to the war ranges all the way from those who believe that a basically sound policy was ineffectively carried out to those who fervently believe that American intervention was completely wrongheaded and malicious and that the Viet Cong deserved to win.

The Future of American Mission

Whatever your own view, you probably share, to some degree, the consensus that the result was failure. Because of that failure, we are now experiencing a great revulsion against the idea that America has any mission in the world. This opposition view goes something like this:

We have no right to impose our way of life on other people. We have no mission in the world. We should have none. Instead of trying to spread American power and influence all over the world, we should devote ourselves to dealing with our own problems. We should end poverty, racism, exploitation, and injustice at home. We should clean up our environment and rebuild our cities. We should build the Good Society right here in America. That will provide a better example for the rest of the world than trying to convert it to our way of thinking.

This is a most persuasive viewpoint, especially in the light of our recent past. But I am not sure it is a repudiation of our concept of the mission of America. Indeed, the idea of mission is so deeply ingrained in our national character that it cannot be expunged simply by the desire to eliminate it. Whether we like it or not, we are an incurably missionary-minded people.

Even when people seem to be saying that we should deal with our own problems exclusively, an implicit missionary assumption may be present. When you ask people who hold this view where such a policy might lead, they usually say something like this:

"Well, if we can build this Good Society at home, we will be showing the world what a Good Society looks like. We will be proving that a free people can provide liberty, justice, and equality. Then maybe the world will be led to imitate what they see."

That is a concept of mission, whether its proponents realize it or not. For the critics of American mission make their criticisms on the basis of a concept of mission, a concept of mission very similar to the original Puritan concept of a city upon a hill. It is close to the Jeffersonian concept of an experiment carried out on behalf of all men who may be led to imitate it.

Such a concept of national mission is legitimate, I believe, if it serves as a source of regeneration, of self-renewal. It need not be pretentious, or aggressive, or coercive. At its best, it can lift us above a pursuit of mere survival, and can link our destiny with that of all men. At the very least, it can force us to consider just what we want our country to be and do.

SUGGESTED READINGS

Ralph H. Gabriel, *The Course of American Democratic Thought* (New York: Ronald Press, 1940, 1956) discusses the concept of American mission as a central category of American thought. Frederick Merk, *Manifest Destiny and Mission in American History* (New York: Alfred A. Knopf, 1963) applies the concept to American foreign policy. The Merk book also contains the quotation from William McKinley. The extract from Thomas Jefferson's letter to Roger C. Weightman can be found in Henry Steele Commager, ed., *Living Ideas in America* (New York: Harper, 1951). The passage from Josiah Strong's *The New Era* is quoted in Sydney Ahlstrom's *Religious History of the American People* (New Haven: Yale University Press, 1972). Martin E. Marty, *Righteous Empire* (New York: Dial, 1970) interprets the nineteenth-century Protestant mission to America. Ray H. Abrams, *Preachers Present Arms* (Washington, D.C.: Round Table Press, 1933) contains an unflattering portrait of the clergymen who vociferously supported America's entrance into the First World War. David M. Potter, *People of Plenty* (Chicago: University of Chicago Press, 1954) discusses the difficulties involved in attempting to export the American version of democratic society.

IV
Freedom—Then and Now

In any discussion of American values the word "freedom" will loom large. Freedom is the granddaddy value of them all. Look at the way in which both liberals and conservatives in America seek to identify their causes with the concept of freedom. During the civil rights movement of the early sixties, the most persistent liberal slogan was "Freedom now!" The activists who rode integrated buses into the South called themselves freedom riders. Freedom schools were operated in black communities when public schools ceased to function. A group of Jewish radicals even published a "Freedom Seder" service for Passover. The related terms "liberty" and "liberation" appear in such names as black liberation, women's liberation, and the American Civil Liberties Union.

At the same time, the leading conservative organization in America calls itself Young Americans for Freedom. The Freedoms Foundation, in Valley Forge, Pennsylvania, presents Freedom Awards annually for significant conservative achievements. And such terms as "the American free enterprise system" and "liberty lobby" suggest that conservatives as well as liberals see themselves as defenders of freedom in America.

Freedom and Authority

The word freedom clearly strikes a responsive chord in the American breast. It is not difficult to see why this should be so. After all, most of the early settlers came to America either to escape from oppression or to look for wider opportunities. Both groups may be said to have been seeking freedom. D. H. Lawrence called America a "vast republic of escaped slaves" more interested in getting away from the old authority of Europe than in seeking genuine freedom.

From the earliest days Americans have tended to resist authority and to move on when it became oppressive. Consider, for example, the Puritans' attempt to build a biblical commonwealth in Massachusetts. They started off with a clear idea of what they wanted to do. They had an articulate theology, a sophisticated blend of reason and emotion. They built a social order and a body of law based on their common commitment to the rule of God. But by the end of the seventeenth century, the whole thing had fallen apart. To run a colony, to attract and hold settlers, they had to ease up on the strictness of their regulated life. Dissenters could always retaliate against authority by going elsewhere, and many did. Pennsylvania, by contrast, was founded on principles of liberality and toleration. As a result, Pennsylvania soon surpassed Massachusetts in population, prosperity, and power. Freedom was already the wave of the future.

Left to themselves, Americans devised their own instruments of government to serve their own perceived needs. Government in the colonies tended to be modest in scope, local in character, personal, manageable, and inexpensive to run. The Americans resisted royal governors, evaded imperial regulations at will, and gradually developed a sense of personal autonomy and a jealous regard for their liberties. The relatively mild assertion of imperial authority by the mother country in the mid-eighteenth century produced anguished cries of "oppression" and "tyranny." Dissent escalated into resistance, violence, and finally, revolution.

After independence was won, the American people were reluctant to give up any of their hard-won liberties, even to their own popularly chosen government. In 1787–88 the proponents of the Constitution faced major opposition in almost every state. To win ratification, they had to promise that a bill of rights would be appended to it when the first Congress met. Those ten amendments form a dramatic assertion of individual rights against government, a fact that has continued to embarrass the advocates of unqualified national power.

A nation founded on an ideal of freedom that limits the scope of government, and whose people deeply believe in their God-given right to do as they please, might be expected to dissolve into chaos in short order. Several of the Founding Fathers—Madison and Hamilton, for example—saw this as a distinct possibility. They believed that the tension between freedom and order constituted the most significant dilemma faced by the new nation.

But things turned out quite otherwise. Until the onset of the Civil War, the antiauthoritarian, freedom-loving Americans seemed relatively docile, patriotic, well-behaved, and law-abiding. Alexis de Tocqueville, writing in the 1830s, observed that it was their religious beliefs that enabled the Americans to maintain their decency, morality, and justice even though the law gave them wider freedom than most men had ever known. As he put it, "while the law permits the Americans to do what they please, religion prevents them from conceiving, and forbids them to commit, what is rash or unjust."

Despite the religious diversity of the early republic, there was a widespread moral consensus that dictated how one ought to act. The mores and customs of the age were enforced by public opinion, perhaps the strongest moral sanction in a democratic society.

Business and Freedom

Economic behavior was also relatively unrestricted in the early nineteenth century. The traditional government practice of granting monopolies to favored enterprises through patents and charters had been successfully opposed by those who demanded the right to compete on an equal footing. As a result, nearly anyone could go into nearly any business without fear of restriction or regulation. Sometimes this unbridled competition produced disaster, both for the entrepreneur and for the public. There were booms and busts, inflations and panics, with alarming regularity. Speculation was rampant, with fortunes made and lost almost casually. But in today's terms, we would have to regard these catastrophes as relatively minor. The enterprises were mostly rather small, and the defeated businessman could usually bounce back and try again.

By the end of the century, things had changed considerably. With the coming of what we now call the urban-industrial age, the scale of economic operations increased enormously. Free enterprise evolved into big business. Instead of swashbuckling entrepreneurs, we had giant corporations, complicated trusts, watered stock, deceptive advertising, labor exploitation. At the same time, a huge and growing polyglot population was living cheek by jowl in the large cities. Traditional social controls began to break down; the amenities of life disappeared. The convictions that had provided moderation and restraint began to wither away. On the economic scene, freedom seemed to produce "malefactors of great wealth." On the social scene, freedom produced vice and immorality.

The response to this new situation was a double-barreled attack on our traditional ideal of freedom, which suddenly seemed out of place in a complex and interdependent world. The attack took different forms, which can conveniently be labeled "liberal" and "conservative," if those words are used in a rather specialized manner. Both liberals and conservatives saw freedom threatened on one front and threatening on another. They disagreed as to which front was which.

In the eyes of liberals, freedom on the economoic front represented a danger to society. Because we had always believed in freedom from government interference, we had been reluctant to regulate the decisions of industrial and commercial enterprises. Indeed, the Supreme Court had determined that corporations, as legal persons, had all the privileges and immunities of actual people and that the Fourteenth Amendment to the Constitution, which was intended to guarantee the liberty of freed Negroes, actually guaranteed the liberty of the corporations.

By the administration of the first Roosevelt, the Progressive party demanded that big business be tamed through government regulation in the interest of the whole society. Federal regulatory agencies were inaugurated, antitrust legislation was rigorously enforced, and government intervention in economic activity became an established fact of our national life.

But not everybody accepted this new direction of government. Businessmen and their conservative allies fiercely resisted what they regarded as the unwarranted encroachment of government into the private lives of its citizens. They appealed to our heritage of private property, limited government, and personal freedom to enlist support for their cause. They invoked Jefferson's libertarian phrase "That government is best which governs least" and called for dismantling of the regulatory agencies. The words freedom and liberty became, in conservative parlance, shorthand for "get the government out of business."

Limitations on Personal Freedom

But if conservatives defended freedom on the economic front, they saw it as a danger in the behavior of the masses. As the urbanization of American society led to the breakdown of social controls, conservatives advocated that traditional mores and customs be sustained by legislation. If men insisted on gambling and drinking, then the law should see that they were punished for their vices. If respect for the Sabbath was breaking down, the law should enforce observation of the Lord's Day. Laws regulated sexual behavior, birth control practices, drug use. As movies grew in popularity, censorship appeared on the scene. Laws against pornography were passed and enforced in order to maintain common decency. Conservatives generally supported these limitations on personal liberty in the name of social stability.

Liberals generally opposed these moves, which they regarded as unwarranted intrusions by government into the private lives of citizens. They fought against censorship in the name of freedom of speech. They fought the Sunday blue laws in the name of freedom of religion. They have proposed wholesale repudiation of laws regulating personal conduct on the ground that such laws create "crimes without victims." Homosexual contact between consenting adults, they maintain, injures no one and should not be regulated by the state. Wiretapping and maintenance of files on noncriminal activity constitutes a dangerous invasion of privacy on the part of the state. In a time of growing governmental power, they assert, the private rights of citizens need to be safeguarded, even at the expense of social stability.

The debate about freedom is still going on. Government is still regulating business, while conservatives protest in the name of free enterprise, and liberals applaud because they believe that only government can maintain economic justice and prevent exploitation by business. Government still regulates individual conduct, censors movies, confiscates pornographic literature, arrests drunks and homosexuals, taps telephones, and keeps files on private citizens. Liberals still protest in the name of free speech and the right to live an unregulated life, while conservatives affirm that government intervention is necessary to maintain decency and to protect the health and morals of the community.

The debate, no doubt, will continue. It has recently been somewhat complicated by the arguments of some liberals and radicals who have come to side with conservatives in opposing the federal regulatory bodies. They claim that government agencies do not really regulate in the public interest. All they do is prevent competition and keep prices high. They are ineffective, unresponsive bureaucracies that should be abolished.

On the other hand, it seems that the complexities of contemporary economic life require more government participation in the regulation of the economy. Commercial products are so complicated that only skilled government inspectors can tell people what they are really buying. Big business and big unions can easily combine to stifle the free choices of private persons. We no doubt need the countervailing power of government at our disposal, even though we do not entirely trust it.

In the private sphere, the past decade has witnessed a massive withdrawal of government from the regulation of private life.

Sunday blue laws have been removed from the books in most places. Movie censorship has been successfully challenged in the courts, and while recent court rulings against pornography may encourage a return of the censor, most observers concede that American society is more open today than it has ever been before.

Dress codes at school and on the job collapsed very quickly once they were seriously challenged. Gone are the days when a boy was sent home from school because he had shoulder-length hair. Laws against fornification and adultery are largely unenforced, and sexual deviation among adults is widely tolerated even where it is still illegal. We seem to be moving toward a society that tolerates a wide variety of life styles, even though it may disapprove of them.

These issues demonstrate the difficulty of upholding our traditional ideal of freedom in a world characterized by bigness, increasing complexity, density, and interdependence. How can we maximize personal freedom without having our society fly apart into chaos and disorder? Some areas of life need to be regulated so that we can live together without disaster. Americans seem to be willing to accept a certain amount of this kind of regulation.

In the debate between the regulators and their opponents, I find myself generally on the side of the libertarians. Like most Americans, I am inherently suspicious of anyone who tells me that I must do something because it's good for me. The Surgeon General's decision to put dire warnings on cigarette packages was a sound one, but if anyone still wants to smoke himself into an early grave, he is free to do so. The decision to ban cyclamates was less acceptable to me. A posted warning, as in the case of cigarettes, would have been quite enough to enable a reasonably prudent man to make an informed choice. The ban takes that choice out of his hands. And while we certainly should applaud the availability of seat belts in automobiles, we have a right to resent having a little buzzer tell us that we can't move the car until we buckle up. If you don't have enough sense to fasten your seat belt, you have the God-given right to go through the windshield. For the powerful, the expert, and the morally superior, this fierce love of freedom makes us seem a stubborn and refractory people. But it's our salvation, and I hope we never lose it.

Negative and Positive Freedom

D. H. Lawrence had a valid point when he claimed that most of those who came to America were running away from something. The result of that early experience has been that for most of us, freedom has been equated with the absence of external restraint. A teen-age girl described this idea of freedom to me many years ago at a youth conference: "I feel like a balloon that's held down by a lot of big, heavy ropes. Freedom is having the ropes off."

That's the American view, but it's an impoverished and inadequate idea of freedom because it's primarily negative. It's freedom *from*, not freedom *to*. Gibson Winter has recently suggested that we need to develop a more positive view of freedom, which he would define as choosing, doing what we want to do, within a framework of lawfulness.

But in a society dominated by complex technology, Winter notes, we are dependent on resources and training for the exercise of liberty. We need, first of all, "freedom to belong." Belonging depends upon access to work, income, medical care, and education. Members of the middle class usually have this access, but unemployment, catastrophic illness, or accident can render anyone helpless. Large-scale economic and political processes leave many powerless and apathetic. A network of support and resources is needed to make freedom meaningful. Only when we have a certain amount of security can we develop the confidence to make our own choices, to initiate our own actions. If we would hold up freedom as an ideal, we need to give people the capacity to use it. Otherwise freedom is only an abstraction that has no effect on life.

Individualism and Community

The idea that freedom requires a supporting society may seem obvious, but it flies in the face of our traditional American equation of freedom with individualism. The most highly prized personality type in America is the autonomous individual. He stands on his own two feet. He asks no favor of any man. He thinks for himself. He is a nonconformist. He moves about freely among all sorts and conditions of men because he is his own man. He knows himself and affirms himself. He says, "I'm OK."

The traditional Christian conception of man tended to contradict this ideal. The Christian was supposed to be humble and obedient. He recognized his dependence on God. He submitted to the authority of the Bible or the church. In practice, he accepted the authority of the minister, who in turn was dependent upon the institutional structures of his denomination. Ministers, in the words of the Prayer Book, were to "set forth" the Word, while the people were to hear and receive it "with meek hearts and due reverence."

Recently the churches have begun to assert the value of personal autonomy and self-direction. Man is called to fashion his own future, and morality is seen as the willingness to take responsibility for it. In screening candidates for the ministry, churches are beginning to weed out dependent personalities and to select people with a high degree of independence and self-confidence. The new and rapidly growing clergy associations are appealing to the clergyman's sense of autonomy and self-worth, insisting that ministers take control of their own professional lives.

There are some pluses and minuses in this development. On the positive side, it fosters people's vitality and makes contact with their potential for growth and maturity. But on the negative side, it leaves us with the problem of community. How can we acknowledge our interdependence? How can we affirm our solidarity?

Because we equate freedom with individualism, we in America have trouble developing an ethic of community. Of couse, community has existed among us, and it has been strong and healthy. But characteristically we are loners. The demands of community life are heard as calls for conformity, which we regard as destructive of authentic personal growth. We may not have invented the conflict between the individual and the community, but we have accepted the dichotomy almost unquestioningly.

The current emphasis on personal autonomy will enrich our lives only if it is accompanied by an equally vigorous affirmation of community. We are, in fact, members one of another, and we ignore it at our peril. We need structures of support in which people can affirm one another, where they can express their real feelings, where they can find acceptance, forgiveness, and reconciliation.

Autonomy and community are not mutually exclusive. For dependent people, community can be a crutch or a hideaway. A community of dependent people can create a neurotic environment that enables its members to evade the truth about themselves. But autonomous people can build community by acknowledging freely the limitations of their own autonomy. Having affirmed themselves, they can affirm others. Standing on their own two feet, they can dare to stand together. Perhaps the contemporary drive toward autonomy will provide us with the tools to build genuine community in the future.

Autonomy has its theological dimension. In Christ, God calls us to freedom. We have been affirmed and can dare to move out of structures, institutions, laws, and traditions. We can make our own decisions and take responsibility for our own lives. We can move out of our isolation and take responsibility for each other; not as officious, authoritarian meddlers who insist on doing good for other people, but as brothers and sisters who share a common destiny.

As St. Paul wrote to the Galatians:

For you were called to freedom, brethren; only do not use your freedom as an opportunity for the flesh, but through love be servants of one another. For the whole law is ful-

filled in one word, "You shall love your neighbor as yourself."
(Gab. 5:13–14)

Once again, we might become what Tocqueville said we were
more than a century ago. We would be a people who have no
need for restrictive laws because we are governed by our own
inner commitments. Not that our religious convictions prevent or
forbid us from wrongdoing, but that our faith has set us free to
be fully autonomous and fully responsible human beings.

The future of freedom in America is both heartening and discouraging. We seem to be learning how to be more self-actual-
izing, autonomous people. That bodes well for the future of personal liberty. But the possibilities of freedom on the large-scale
level of social, economic, and political structures are a tougher
problem. Our institutions can enslave us or they can make us
free. Today we fear their capacity for oppression more than we
prize their ability to confer freedom. This may change in the
years to come, but it will change only if our institutions are penetrated by great numbers of men and women whose faith has set
them free, who have learned how to work together to effect
change in their environment. They are the salt of the earth. If
we are lucky, there may be enough salt to go around.

SUGGESTED READINGS

D. H. Lawrence's remarks about Americans are found in his
Studies in Classic American Literature (first published 1923;
paperback: New York: Viking Compass edition, 1964). The classic
debate on the place of freedom in the economic system can be
followed by reading Friedrich A. Hayek, *The Road to Serfdom*
(Chicago: University of Chicago Press, 1944), who equates economic planning with totalitarianism and calls for the play of free
market forces. He was answered in *Road to Reaction* (Boston:
Little, Brown, 1946), by Herman Finer, who took the position
that responsible planning under democratic auspices is necessary
to provide the economic security that makes freedom possible.
Barry Goldwater carries Hayek's views into his political thinking

in *The Conscience of a Conservative* (New York: Macfadden-Bartell, 1960). Gibson Winter's view of the place of freedom in a technological society is presented in *Being Free* (New York: Macmillan, 1970). Thomas A. Harris, *I'm OK—You're OK* (New York: Harper & Row, 1969; paperback: Avon, 1973) states the case for the autonomous self-directed personality. Harvey Cox in his recent work, *Seduction of the Spirit* (New York: Simon & Schuster, 1973), applies the idea of a theology of liberation to the role of religion in contemporary culture.

V

Equality:

INCLUSION, OPPORTUNITY, DIVERSITY

Americans believe deeply in the principle of equality. We take great pride in our Declaration of Independence, which states it to be a self-evident truth that "all men are created equal." We boast that in our society, you are judged by what you are, not who you are, or who your parents were. For many Americans, equality is our most important national value.

Our ideal of equality is important to the rest of the world as well. Of all our values and goals, equality is the one other nations have heard most about, and the one by which they judge us—usually unfavorably. Once foreign visitors have gotten past the politeness barrier, they nearly always bring up the gap between our commitment to equality as an ideal and our actual performance. "You preach equality," they point out, "but you don't practice it." Unfortunately they are right. Nowhere is the distance so great between the promise of American life and its actuality.

But despite our failure to achieve equality, it still ranks high as a shared value. When confronted with the facts about inequality, most conscientious Americans feel guilty about our shortcomings. We recognize the persistence of inequalities as a fault, a failure, a promise to be solved, an injustice to be corrected. Martin Luther King knew this. His appeals for racial justice were always couched in the language of Scripture and the Declaration of Independence. Fair-minded people could see and accept what he was saying because they recognized their own values in his sermons and speeches. When confronted with the disparity between those values and the actualities of prejudice, discrimination, and legal segregation, most Americans supported major changes in legislation and even in their customary behavior.

But a sensitive observer might ask—and many foreign visitors have asked—why have we allowed two hundred years to elapse since the Declaration of Independence without fully implementing the ideals it set forth so persuasively? Why is there still discrimination against black people, Indian Americans, chicanos, and others? Why are women still fighting for equality?

Our answers are more likely to be explanations than justifications. We could say that we Americans have set our sights very high. We have aimed at a level of equality that no society has ever come close to achieving, so it is not surprising that we have not got there yet.

We could also say that most Americans are unaware, most of the time, of the nature and extent of the inequalities that exist around us. You don't have to be blind or deaf, or a vicious racist, or a totally insensitive clod, to miss the degradations that go on around you, just out of sight. I can remember, for example, my own reaction to the Supreme Court school-desegregation decision of 1954. I was then a student in a theological seminary. I had graduated from college with a degree in political science and had served in the army, two years of that time in the Deep South. I had been raised in an integrated neighborhood, had worked in a variety of occupations, and regarded myself as a rather enlightened political liberal, kindly disposed toward my fellow man. Yet I can distinctly remember my reaction to the Supreme Court decision as I read the newspaper that day. It was: "Well, that problem is solved, thank God."

I can see now that I had no real idea of the extent of racism in our society, or of the powerful forces allied with the system as it then existed. It took the ferment and dislocations of the next decade to educate me about the real plight of the black American. I suspect that the same was true of many other white Americans.

The Legacy of Inequality

Equality is a relatively new idea. It was not part of our original
cultural heritage but came on the scene rather late in our history.
While the earliest colonial settlers had a concern for freedom,
they had no commitment to equaity. Whether Puritan or Vir-
ginian, Englishman or German, the settler came from a highly
stratified society. Ideas of rank and privilege were enshrined in
the laws and the customs of the Old World. Inequality was sanc-
tioned by the Christian religion, whether Protestant or Catholic.
Christians believed that God loves all men, but they also believed
that God himself created the differences of birth and rank that
enabled each man to know his place in the social order. They
believed that God requires each man to do his duty "in that state
of life to which it hath pleased God to call him." They believed
that the king should be happy and revered in his palace; the
peasant should be happy and secure in his cottage. But none of
this nonsense about equality. Not in this world.

When settlers arrived in the New World, the old distinctions
were not easily laid aside. The Puritans, for example, adopted
laws that prescribed the dress appropriate to various ranks of
society. An artisan could be severely punished for wearing the
garb of a gentleman. For a time, colleges listed graduates according to rank. Even in the churches, the congregations were seated
according to the social standing of the various families.

But changes began to take place at an early date in the Eng-
lish-speaking colonies. For one thing, most settlers were common-
ers, since nobles had little incentive to emigrate. America never
had a tradition favoring hereditary titles. There were social distinctions, of course, but they were tied to wealth, land, and pro-
fession. There was no feeling that wealthy people were somehow
"better" than others. People could too easily remember that the
rich and pretentious merchant had a grandfather who made bar-
rels and perhaps used to drink a little too much. Even in the
South, the large plantation owner was likely to be related to
numbers of poor country folk.

Conditions in the American colonies made egalitarian practice likely and the ideal of equality reasonable. But equality was in the air on the other side of the Atlantic too. The rising middle classes in the commercial centers of Europe were bidding for their place in the sun. They resented the laws and customs that gave the hereditary nobility the chief places in the court, while restricting the social and political activities of self-made men like themselves. In France the cry came to be for "a career open to talent," while in England, the Levellers and Diggers of the English Civil War period asserted the equality of the least Englishman with the greatest.

What is now called the Enlightenment was a broad-gauged social and intellectual movement that reinforced and disseminated these ideas. Writers such as Voltaire and Rousseau in France and Locke and Shaftesbury in England developed doctrines of natural rights that were intended to apply to all men. The church, unfortunately whether Protestant or Catholic, did little to assert the ideas of equal rights. Most of the established churches accepted the values of the old order: rank, status, hierarchy. Many of the leaders of organized religion vigorously opposed the newer democratic ideas on the ground that they promoted atheism and social strife. Only religious radicals such as Anabaptists, Quakers, and Unitarians were likely to espouse the doctrine of equality—at least until the American Revolution.

Equality, then, is a value that made its way slowly but surely in the American environment. It was not part of our "original" inheritance—if we go back to the seventeenth-century settlers—but the conditions of life on the new continent provided an environment in which the idea of equality could take hold and spread. By the time of the Revolution, it was a value widely shared among Americans, supported by their experience, and justified by numerous philosophers of the Enlightenment. By our standards, both the theory and practice of equality in the eighteenth century were narrow, restricted, and inadequate.

There are two aspects of the question of equality in America: inclusion and meaning. First, we must decide who is entitled to equality, as our concept of those to whom equality pertains has changed over the years. That is the question of inclusion. Second, we must discuss the meanings of equality, for equality has had many meanings in America, and not all of us can agree on its meaning today.

The Issue of Inclusion

Americans have constantly expanded their conception of who is entitled to equality. We can point with some pride to progress. Though we have come a long way, we still have a long way to go.

Today it seems incredible that Thomas Jefferson could compose a Declaration of Independence containing the statement

> We hold these truths to be self-evident, that all men are created equal, that they are endowed by their Creator with certain unalienable Rights, that among these are Life, Liberty, and the Pursuit of Happiness . . .

and at the same time own slaves. He even had a personal slave in attendance while he was writing the Declaration. To be fair to Jefferson, I must add that he was conscious of the irony. He worried about the condition of the slaves. He even speculated about the Negro's potential for freedom, and about the Indian's as well. But for both Indian and Negro, Jefferson, like most of his contemporaries, assumed a separate social existence. When the Founding Fathers declared that "all men" were created equal, they meant, in practice, all white males.

Actually, not even all white males could vote in the new nation, even after the Revolution. In most places, there was still a property qualification for the right to vote, based on the conservative principle that only those with a property interest in the society should have the right to decide how that society should be run. But the logic of equality undercut this line of reasoning, and by the time Andrew Jackson became president, most of those qualifications had disappeared.

Women

As far as women were concerned, it is not precisely true to say that they were not included in the idea of equality. American women, even in the early nineteenth century, were among the freest women in the world. They did not have to put up with the petty restrictions commonly placed on women in the aristocratic societies of France and Spain. They could dress pretty much to their own taste. They could move about quite freely. Indeed, it was said that a woman could travel alone from one end of the country to the other in perfect safety, certain that she would always receive respectful treatment, even from the roughest of men. Young girls moved about in society and commonly spoke quite freely in mixed company.

What are perceived by us as injustices and inequities enforced upon women were seldom so perceived at the time, mainly because women in America were considered well off by comparison with their counterparts in the rest of the world. From our perspective, the disabilities are obvious. Women could not vote. It was difficult for women to hold property. They were barred from most forms of employment. They were denied equal access to education. They were put on a pedestal, but at the same time were locked into a sharply defined social role. Even where the laws were silent, community standards were quite clear as to what women were and were not to do.

But as the nineteenth century wore one, the role of women in American society underwent vast changes. Women moved into traditional masculine occupations such as teaching, nursing, and later clerical and secretarial work in the business world. They came to dominate these occupations to such an extent that today we normally think of them as "women's work." Educational opportunities opened up on all levels, and coeducation got under way and soon became the dominant mode of education in America. The political bastions were the last to fall, with women's suffrage coming very late—far later than in some European countries. Even after the right to vote was gained, it was the unusual woman who went so far as to seek public office.

These changes in the position of women came slowly, often painfully, and in the face of significant opposition from women as well as men. It was not that the opponents wanted to keep women in an inferior position, but that they had clear ideas as to what constituted women's proper role. They saw women as developing a "separate but equal" status alongside—and perhaps a little behind—men.

The 1920s saw the most significant shift in the position of women, when, after suffrage, they moved into more and more jobs, adopted more casual dress styles and behavior patterns, experimented with sexual freedom, sought careers, drove cars, smoked cigarettes, and drank whiskey in public. By 1946, when servicemen returned from World War II looking for wives, families, and jobs, many young women were ready to turn their backs on careers in favor of home and motherhood. "Rosie the Riveter" was quickly discarded as a model for the patriotic American woman. The new model was the family marketing expert. To sell soap, cleansers, cosmetics, clothes, and baby food, the advertising media developed the "feminine mystique," which kept women preoccupied with their personal appearance and their maternal and domestic roles.

The current women's movement is a predictable reaction. Women once again are asserting their ability to handle any job a man can do. They are demanding equal pay for equal work. They are expressing resentment at being regarded as slightly less than complete human beings. The movement is deeply divided, however, on the issue of what a woman really is.

Some of the more radical spokeswomen would maintain that there are no fundamental differences between men and women, aside from those associated with reproduction and nursing. Other differences are culturally determined, these women assert, and can be eliminated by changes in the way children are reared and educated. All nonbiological differences should be eliminated so that people can be people first, men and/or women second. All individuals should have the right to choose their sexual roles to suit themselves.

I can't accept this view myself because I'm convinced that a culture that does not provide enough clues to enable a boy or girl to identify himself/herself sexually will leave its young people hopelessly confused and demoralized. To be sure, we need to loosen up our conceptions of sex roles. We need to affirm the women who want professional careers as well as those who want homes and children. We need to let the young know the full range of options that lie before them. But to go further and teach—by precept or example—that there are no fundamental differences between men and women would be to set in motion cultural dislocations that would have wide-ranging side effects that few of us can even foresee. In this area, as in many others, we have to be able to distinguish between equality and uniformity.

Racism

The women's movement has, through the years, been led primarily by women who themselves have felt oppressed by the roles into which society cast them. The movement for racial justice and equality has had a different history. Early efforts to free blacks and improve their lot were led and shaped by white people. Only recently have black Americans had enough social standing and political power to provide leadership for their own liberation movement.

Racism is by all odds the area where our failure to achieve equality in American society has been most destructive. On a simple-minded level, it is clear that the black, like the Indian, has been subjugated because it has been in someone's economic interest to keep him on the bottom of the heap. The slaveholder, of course, profited from the forced labor of his slaves. The pioneer farmers who settled the West profited from the frequent breaking of treaties with the Indians that led to confiscation of good lands and resettlement of the tribes farther west on poorer lands. Today many white workers profit from the fact that blacks are effectively excluded from competing for jobs in their craft or trade.

It has clearly been racism that has kept black people on the bottom for so long. Most immigrant groups have suffered from discrimination based on their perceived inferiority. In the early nineteenth century, every employer knew for certain that Irishmen were unfit for citizenship in a free republic. They made poor workmen. They were lazy and unreliable. They drank too much whisky. They gambled. They had a high crime rate. They were given to violence, both on and off the job. Hence any self-respecting employer felt quite free to post a sign that read: "No Irish Need Apply."

But in spite of such discrimination, the Irish made it. They finally won the jobs, the schooling, the economic advancement that enabled them to become assimilated into American society. And after them, one immigrant group after another made it and gradually became absorbed until they lost any sense of a separate identity.

But the black was not so fortunate. Even after slavery was ended, his color made him a marked man. As late as 1900, Jacob Riis could point to the urban Negro of New York as superior to the "white foreigner" in cleanliness and orderliness, but still, he noted, the Negro was the victim of conscious and unapologetic discrimination in housing. There was theory behind the practice. The Negro was regarded as a member of an inferior race, so the tradition of equality could not of course apply to him.

This is a point that deserves emphasis. Racism was ingrained in American society, not only because it served some men's economic interests, not only because sinful men treated their fellow men in ways that contradicted their own values, but also because the doctrine of racial inequality was backed by the prestige of science. The theory that mankind is divided into various races, some superior and others inferior, was accepted by the best scientific minds of the time.

While doing research for another book, I had reason to look for all the material I could find on the idea of racial equality in the nineteenth century. Every reference to race assumed theories of inequality. I was unable to find any body of scientific opinion that advanced the concept of racial equality before the end of the century. In other words, racism was not merely an emotional bias of red-necks and reactionaries. It was the consensus of the social science community as well as of the general public. No wonder society was shot through with discriminatory practices that made a mockery of the Declaration of Independence.

This view was shared even by most friends of the Negro, including those who worked hardest for black education, political rights, and social betterment. White liberals honestly desired to improve the lot of blacks, but they had no confidence in his ability to achieve genuine equality with themselves. We need not accuse these reformers of bad faith. They merely shared the beliefs of their time.

The only people who did not share this view were the blacks themselves. It is a remarkable testimony to the inherent dignity of the human spirit that a few articulate leaders of the Negro community could steadfastly maintain the equality of their people in the face of an almost unbroken consensus against that view. Yet men like Frederick Douglass and, later, W. E. B. Du Bois ridiculed the theories of the ideologues of racism in terms that makes their writings stand out far ahead of their times.

It was not until this century that opinion in the social sciences leaned toward the doctrine of racial equality. Today the conviction is almost universal. Many anthropologists would go further and maintain that the concept of race is so vague and confused as to be meaningless as an analytical tool. But it has taken more than half a century for that view to take hold in the mind of the general public to the extent that it has begun to reshape our social institutions.

This, I believe, is the real meaning of the civil rights movement of the fifties and sixties. While it would be naïve to say today, as I said in 1954, that the race problem is "solved," nevertheless, I am convinced that the backbone of racism within our social structures has been broken. The logic of equality is beginning to work its way through our institutional life, into our

personal value systems. The inherited behavior patterns and
value systems of centuries are not about to change overnight,
but change is clearly on the way.

One factor favoring change is that the black community now
generates its own leadership, its own agents for change. Black
leaders have a clearer perception of the needs and wants of their
own communities than did the white leadership of previous generations. Moreover, the sight of capable, articulate, and effective
black professionals provides support for the concept of equality
among whites and blacks. Thousands of Americans who have
heretofore seen black people only as janitors, laborers, or house-
maids are now getting a different picture of what it means to
be black.

Retarding change, however, is the accumulation of inherited
disabilities—economic, educational, cultural—that cannot easily
be overcome by altering individual attitudes or legislating new
federal programs. The economic rise of black people is inhibited
by the fact that most of the good spots in the economy are already taken. The black is competing at a serious disadvantage.
Starting off poorer, he finds it harder to get the educational
credentials that admit him to a better job. Relegated to the outside, he consequently has to think and act like an outsider.

This, of course, is the reason why many social critics favor
"catch-up" programs: benign quotas in schools and jobs; busing
to achieve racial integration; affirmative action programs to en-
sure that black people get first crack at jobs formerly denied
them. Such proposals have stirred a storm of controversy because they seem to deny the idea of equality. To discriminate
in favor of the poor or the black seems as unjustifiable as discriminating against them. Given these contradictions, how can a
racist society turn itself around and achieve genuine racial
equality? Some value has to give.

The Meaning of Equality

Our pursuit of equality has been complicated by the fact that
we do not always agree about what we mean by equality. Do

we mean, for example, equality of opportunity or equality of condition?

Throughout most of our history, we have favored the former: equality has meant that an individual should suffer no artificial impediments to success. He should have the right to go as far as his energy, intelligence, resourcefulness, and dedication could carry him. If that meant that some men ended up as millionaires and others as paupers, well, there was no great harm done. The pauper might have made his millions had he properly applied himself.

Up to a point, this version of equality produced a rough equality of condition. Before the age of industrialism, there were a few very rich Americans, but not many. And while there was some poverty, most of it was either the temporary poverty of the recent arrival or the poverty of the inadequate and incompetent. The richness of resources, the availability of land, and the shortage of manpower combined to produce a general prosperity and reduce the incidence of poverty. In their comments on American life, European travelers often noted this with approval.

In such a society, the poor seldom envied, hated, or feared the rich. They did not support political movements devoted to leveling incomes. Even after industrialization, the United States never developed a mass political movement based on socialism. Unions have concentrated on increasing workers' wages, not on expropriating the capitalists or soaking the rich. The poor man would want to go easy on the rich because he harbored the hope that someday he might be one of the rich himself. And if not himself, then surely his children.

Most nonrich Americans don't believe that any more. Our resources no longer seem limitless. We are faced with a drastic energy shortage that will certainly put a crimp in our economy for the next decade, at the most optimistic estimate. We no longer have a labor shortage, but rather an oversupply. It takes a lot of money to make money. Opportunity does not seem as readily available as it once did. For this reason, many social analysts believe that in order to maintain genuine and meaningful equality, those at the upper end of the income scale are going to have to pay more to support the aspirations of those at the bottom.

Equality now means access to jobs and income, guaranteed by public policy. If society can't provide a person with a job, he deserves to be guaranteed an income. He needs sufficient education to qualify for a job, medical care, and an adequate pension when he grows old. He needs protection against economic calamity over which he has no control. All these benefits require immense economic resources, which means heavier taxation, especially of those who can best afford it. Equality has increasingly come to mean equality of condition.

There is something to be said for this view. No one would seriously argue that everybody ought to exist at the same economic level. But it seems to me that the enormous disparity of wealth and income in America today makes a mockery of the idea of equality. While many Americans are buying their second home and their third automobile, others lack a decent place to live. While some Americans diet, others starve. We could stand to move a long way toward equality of condition without leveling the society to the point where initiative is destroyed.

Uniformity or Diversity

The very first group of settlers shared a common English cultural heritage. But early in colonial times, Pennsylvanians were confronted with the arrival of "Dutch" immigrants. These newcomers—actually Germans—preferred to use their own language. When other groups with different life styles and languages reached America, old settlers wondered whether the new nation would speak one common tongue or be a multilingual state. Would these varieties be assimilated into a single American breed?

The language question was answered, though not to everyone's satisfaction, by requiring the use of English in the emerging public school system. But the basic questions would not stay settled. Should "different" population groups follow their separate destinies or be incorporated into the American "mainstream"? That question has been posed over and over again, by various groups, in every generation.

The two possibilities are assimilation and cultural pluralism. The assimilationists see America as "the melting pot." This metaphor suggests that American society is a giant caldron, in which national, racial, and cultural differences are eliminated and a common American type is produced. Native Americans who conducted "Americanization" classes for newly arrived immigrants adhered to this view, though they seldom spelled it out. Immigrants who tried hard to adopt standard American dress, manners, language, and ideas also believed in the melting pot, though they may never have heard the term.

But the pot never completely melted everyone down to the identical brand of Americana. In the 1950s, sociologist Will Herberg suggested that we really had a "transmuting pot," which broke down the old national identities but transformed them into religious identities. America, he maintained, was a tripartite community consisting of Protestants, Catholics, and Jews.

In recent years, however, we have seen a surprising reaffirmation of ethnicity on the part of many subgroups in American society. Perhaps the black-power movement started it all, as militant young leaders of the black community called for separate development and a reassertion of black cultural values. They made it clear that they didn't want to be assimilated into a white racist society that would require them to give up their cultural heritage in order to participate.

It wasn't long before Indians were asserting red power, and Irish were calling for green power. Italian power and Polish power came soon after. Books such as Michael Novak's *The Rise of the Unmeltable Ethnics* appeared, proclaiming that ethnic identity was still an important value for many Americans.

This is a call for cultural pluralism. It is a vision of a multinational, multiracial society that preserves the uniqueness of each heritage while affirming the unity of all. It takes every man seriously in terms of his own heritage and says, in effect, that his particularities are OK, that they have a legitimate place in American society, that he need not conform to a standard American type.

This viewpoint affirms the value of our diversity as a people, and that's important. But assimilation and interaction are still the primary facts of American life. It would be a mistake to think that strong and self-conscious national, racial, or religious groups will persist in our future. The melting pot hasn't completed its work, but it is still melting.

Most Americans can find a mixture of racial and ethnic roots at the base of their family tree. Moreover, the rate of intermarriage is increasing rapidly in America. Interfaith weddings, both Protestant/Catholic and Jewish/Christian, are on the rise, in spite of the objections of the major religious communities. Interracial marriages no longer provoke much surprise or comment in metropolitan areas. I am convinced that the pot is melting today faster than ever before. And I am just as convinced that the process will continue. Ethnicity serves a temporary purpose as a hedge against uniformity, but it is only a way station to a future in which our ethnic backgrounds will be so thoroughly mixed that they will become meaningless to most Americans.

But this does not mean that Americans will develop into a uniform population. Far from it. We can already see new forms of diversity emerging as fast as the old ones disappear. For example, there is much talk among the young concerning "alternative life styles," accompanied by experimentation with new kinds of family structures, schooling, food-buying clubs, communes, diets, etc. It may be that none of these particular efforts is the wave of the future, but they do illustrate the diversity of options that lies before us. In the American future, most people will have increased freedom to choose among many alternatives: in the way they dress, the way they live, the entertainment they enjoy, the values they hold. Uniformity is simply not in the cards for us as a people.

The Future of Equality

If we take all these factors into consideration, then, where do we as a nation stand with respect to our traditional value of equality?

We are continuing to broaden the range of inclusion. We can hope that within the foreseeable future no American will suffer from discrimination on the basis of race, creed, or sex. We still have glaring inequities in wealth and income, and there is no sign that the gaps between the richest and the poorest are being closed. If we want to achieve anything even remotely resembling equality of condition, we will have to make that issue a matter of major national priority. I do not see this happening.

The issue of racism is perhaps the most persistent sore on the body social. While we have eliminated some of its worst manifestations, it remains to be seen whether our inherited racial attitudes have undergone significant change. If equality is to become a meaningful reality, then racism in all its forms will have to disappear. Unlike America, most of the nations of the world are not made up of white majorities. For the nonwhite world, with which we do business and exchange ideas, our racial attitudes and behavior will provide the test of our sincerity about the value of equality.

SUGGESTED READINGS

Daniel Boorstin, *The Lost World of Thomas Jefferson* (Boston: Beacon Press, 1960) discusses Jefferson's soul-searching over the matter of Negro equality. Jacob Riis described the casual but callous discrimination against Negro tenants in *How the Other Half Lives* (New York: Charles Scribner's Sons, 1890), now available in a number of paperback editions. Gunnar Myrdal's classic study of the place of the Negro in American society is *An American Dilemma* (New York: Harper, 1944). The two volume 20th anniversary edition, *American Dilemma: The Negro Problem and Modern Democracy* is available in paperback. Myrdal sees the dilemma as the conflict between the

American ideals of liberty and equality and the inferior status actually accorded the Negro in America. Michael Novak, *The Rise of the Unmeltable Ethnics* (New York: Macmillan, 1972) is only one of a number of recent works extolling the persistence of ethnic identity in America. Will Herberg, *Protestant—Catholic —Jew* (Garden City, N.Y.: Doubleday, 1960) stated his view that religious identity had replaced ethnic identity for hyphenated Americans. Sociologists today regard his view less sympathetically now that religious identity seems to be assuming less and less importance. An excellent group of essays discussing equality from a number of perspectives is J. Roland Pennock and John W. Chapman, eds., *Equality* (New York: Atherton Press, 1967).

VI

Meeting the Mystery of Grace

Americans have always been an optimistic people. In the words of General Electric's advertising slogan, "Progress is our most important product." Change is our oldest tradition. We usually expect that change will be for the better. As a result, we encourage change, support it, approve it, and brag about it. Back in the days when small-town boosterism was a national disease, it was not uncommon to see a sign along the roadside that read: "Elmtown, pop. 543. Watch us grow!" Growth, change, progress —these words have served as symbols of America's abiding faith in the future.

This has not been an abstract faith. It has been expressed in concrete, particular terms. Most Americans throughout most of our history have been confident that our children will be better off than we: be better educated, have better jobs, earn more money, enjoy a higher standard of living, own more possessions, enjoy better health, live more comfortable lives in a better society.

With such a vision before them, the very poorest Americans have been inspired to work and save for the sake of the future. Their expectation has enabled them to endure the sufferings and dangers of the present with relatively little anger or indignation. The result has been that the promise of the future has contributed to the stability of American society. As noted earlier, Americans have not been given to class antagonism primarily because even the poor have harbored the hope that they too— or at least their children—might someday be numbered among the wealthy and privileged.

The Ground of American Optimism

We have put our faith in the future, and the future, on the whole, has delivered the goods. The incredibly tiny, struggling colonial settlements caught hold, expanded, and began to prosper. Southern planters began to sell tobacco at a good price and used their profits to acquire more land. Northern merchants carried their goods to the West Indies and on to England, amassing significant profits in money. The small farms of the South grew into large plantations, while the small trading companies of the North grew into wealthy houses of commerce.

Not everyone became rich, but even the middling sort of folk prospered in their own way. Those who could not afford to pay their own passage to America could sign indentures, or contracts, binding them to serve for up to seven years in return for their passage. After these common laborers had served their time, many became small independent farmers or artisans. With enough hard work and self-discipline, they were able to reach a level of affluence that would have been far beyond their reach back in England.

The process that sociologists designate by the colorless term "upward mobility" continued throughout the nineteenth century. Immigrants by the millions landed at the East Coast cities, often with no possessions other than the clothes they wore or what they could pack in a carpet bag. Some were lucky enough to go west and obtain land—even free land, under the Homestead Act. Their life was not an easy one, as Jan Troell has recently shown us in his two powerful films *The Emigrants* and *The New Land*. They worked long hours; they worked incredibly hard; they endured privation and poverty for years on end. But sooner or later, they managed to pay off the mortgages, build better houses, educate their children, which sometimes meant that the children left the farms to find better opportunities in the cities.

The immigrants who stayed in the cities often had to endure even harder conditions. They worked in sweatshops; they lived in tenements; they put up with filth and disease and exploitation.

Yet they too were often able to see their children acquire new skills, obtain better jobs, get some schooling at public expense, and move into the middle class.

Not everyone prospered, of course. But enough people did at least improve their condition to inspire widespread confidence that hard work, thrift, and self-discipline would pay off. In the midst of the misery and exploitation, a man could still believe that if you kept faith with the future, the future would keep faith with you.

The Idea of Progress

America's continued growth and prosperity was seen as proof of the idea of progress, the belief that the world was getting better and would continue to do so. The American's reading of history led him to this conclusion. He saw kings and empires replaced by democratic governments, arbitrary power replaced by the rule of law. The common man was becoming aware of his own inherent dignity and significance. Labor-saving machinery was taking the drudgery out of work. Brutality and inhumanity were denounced by reformers, and surely it would only be a matter of time before reason and compassion would prevail.

The idea of progress was supported by the new doctrine of evolution. Darwinism seemed to give the sanction of science to the belief that the world was getting better and wiser. If, as men now believed, the fittest survive, isn't the survivor the better man, and doesn't his survival guarantee the improvement of the species? The application of evolutionary notions to the movement of society not only supported the idea of progress but, as interpreted by its most enthusiastic adherents, seemed to make progress inevitable. Perhaps the ultimate statement of this viewpoint came in the 1920s, when thousands of Americans repeated the formula proposed by the French pop psychologist Émile Coué: "Every day in every way I am getting better and better."

The idea of progress was for many a secular substitute for

religious faith, but it had its roots in religious tradition nonetheless. The Pilgrims, for example, believed that since God had called them, he would take care of them. In their early years here, when a drought was broken by plentiful rains after their fervent prayers, they were convinced that God had shown his approval of their project.

Those early New England Calvinists were not so crass as to believe that wealth in itself was a sign of God's favor. Their view of human wickedness was too realistic to permit them to accept such a simplistic conclusion. But as the whole nation prospered through the years, Americans found it easy to believe that God was somehow especially well disposed toward us. Christians could believe that God's providence was manifested in the American commonwealth. They thought that they saw in American history the gradual unfolding of God's divine plan for mankind. Thus a religious version of the doctrine of progress grew up alongside the secular version.

The Age of Disillusionment

Our assumptions about progress, religious or secular, have been deeply shaken by the experiences of our more recent history. Early in this century, men such as Walter Rauschenbusch, the "theologian of the social gospel," looked at the exploitation and dehumanization that accompanied the coming of urban-industrial society and doubted that peaceful progress would be possible in the future. The dislocations of our society, he feared, would work themselves out only through upheaval and violence.

The experience of the twentieth century has reinforced our uncertainty about the future. We have lived through two cataclysmic world wars. We have witnessed the development of superweapons: atomic and hydrogen bombs, intercontinental ballistic missiles, poison gas, napalm, and defoliants. We have lived with dangerous international tensions throughout most of our lives. We have had to face the question of whether mankind itself will survive.

Our domestic experience leads us to parallel doubts. In spite of our prosperity, we seem unable to eradicate poverty in our midst. In spite of our commitment to justice and equality, we have been revealed to be a racist society. A generation of affluence has brought us unrest, domestic violence, and a persistent sense of malaise. Prosperity and power, we have learned, do not bring us peace and happiness.

As we look toward the future, we are confronted with the growing recognition that we are doing irreversible damage to the physical fabric of our world. We are using up natural resources so fast that we are in danger of running short of them unless we cut back on our rate of consumption. And as we use up our fuel supply, we dump the residues into the air and water, causing damage that we may not be able to repair. Whereas technology was once seen as the savior that would provide solutions for our problems, it is seen today as the major hazard to our future.

With all these factors brought forcibly to our consciousness, it is no wonder that our traditional American optimism has begun to fade. Our best minds, our most sensitive people, our most perceptive analysts look at our future and are alarmed. The newspapers, magazines, and television focus on the depth of our concern about the future. The signs are everywhere. The word optimist is commonly preceded by the adjective "naïve." If you regard yourself as an optimist, you find yourself apologizing for the fact. The word realist has come to be equated with pessimist. People no longer write utopias. We have invented a new literary form: the antiutopia, the vision of a disastrous future. Books such as Orwell's *1984* and Huxley's *Brave New World* are symptomatic of our generation's view of the future. Even B. F. Skinner's *Walden II*, intended to depict utopia, is more likely to suggest hell to the average American reader.

Aside from changes in our attitudes, we are also seeing significant changes in public policies that relate to the future. When Congress voted not to fund a supersonic transport plane, it made the first break in our historic policy of support for every feasible technological development. Heretofore we have always assumed that if a thing could be done, it should be done. Now there are strong national movements for zero population growth, for a no-growth economic policy, for countering the effects of rapid economic development. In some localities, no-growth policies have won victories at the polls. It is something new for Americans to vote against growth and change in their communities in the interest of preserving the future.

All these phenomena can be seen as straws in the wind and they all drift in the same general direction. They point to a loss of faith in the future, a loss of the traditional American optimism that we, and the rest of the world, have assumed to be our characteristic attitude toward the future. We are coming to adopt a gloomy outlook because we suspect that our present problems may be overwhelming our future possibilities.

Optimism, Pessimism, and Faith

What is the faithful Christian to make of all this? What does our religious heritage suggest to us in our new situation? Does the Christian tradition support our optimism—or our pessimism?

A clear perception of where the world is heading must, I believe, undercut any genuine optimism. We are in a time when if you are not alarmed, you just don't understand the situation. The dangers we face are real, and our capacity to meet them is in doubt. When you add up social instability, economic dislocations, international insecurity, population pressures, resource depletion, and environmental deterioration, you are left with little ground for optimism.

Christian faith does not define our attitude toward such issues, but it does call us to be clear about the facts. It is hard to see how any sensitive and perceptive reading of the facts can lead us to a sunny outlook. Today's Christian is not likely to be an optimist.

But pessimism is not an inevitable alternative. The pessimist may have the facts on his side, but he has little else. For the pessimist is one who has given up on the future. He does not see the possibility of any new things, any unexpected change, any means of grace. For the pessimist, the wickedness and stupidity of man seem to overcome the power and goodness of God. He has lost faith in both God and man. He has allowed his perception of evil to obscure the possibility of alternative futures.

The faithful Christian would claim that beyond both optimism and pessimism lies hope. Hope encompasses both optimism and pessimism but is itself more than either one.

Christian hope is based on faith in the God who called Abraham out of his comfortable homeland into an unknown future. He is the God who presented himself to Israel in the wilderness as a pillar of cloud by day and a pillar of fire by night. He is the God who led the Pilgrims across a dangerous ocean to a still more dangerous destination. He is the God who calls us today to risk our unknown future, but who promises to be with us as we go. He is the God of the open future, who calls us to work with him in shaping that future into his kingdom.

Those who have heard the call of the Lord in the past and who have followed him in faith have had to shake loose from much that is familiar and beloved. For them, the going has often been hard and discouraging. They have suffered loss, poverty, exile, pain, and death. They have not always reached the promised destination. The call to the future is not a sure-fire guarantee of success.

The Mystery of Grace

But there have been those times when the faithful have found grace, the sense of being supported, the sense of an abiding confidence, the sense of being fulfilled and justified. Grace is the mystery that sustains the faithful in the midst of the unknown. It is the source of the hope that inspires courage and fortitude, that keeps us going when the going is especially rough, our bearings are uncertain, and the goal seems very far away.

The grace of God has surely been manifested in our history. We have been blessed with a bountiful land, a set of essentially sound institutions of government, relative freedom from war and devastation, economic prosperity, and moderate ease and comfort. While we have frequently been bedazzled with our own success, while we are often in danger of losing our way, while we have repeatedly betrayed our own best convictions, we have survived as a people. We have not been overtaken by disaster, and we have managed, through war, depression, and corruption, to hold fast to some of our central values, preserving the seeds of renewal that may still serve us in the future. Even in the midst of evils that we must admit, and sins that we must confess, we can hold to the faith that, in us and through us, and sometimes in spite of us, God's will shall be done.

This sort of conviction enabled Abraham Lincoln to dedicate the cemetery at Gettysburg in the midst of a devastating civil war with the call to "a new birth of freedom." If we believe that God still watches over human history, that he will prevail in spite of our sins and weakness, then we can find grace in the midst of peril, confusion, and adversity. That is the ground of our hope.

To be faithful, then, means to move into the future in the conviction that God himself goes before to meet us with the mystery of his grace. We are called to keep moving so that we can keep up with him. We are not called to be naïve optimists who refuse to face the worst that lies ahead. Nor are we called to be cynical pessimists who refuse to consider any new and fresh possibilities. We are called to be a pilgrim people, a people of faith and hope, who believe in a God who is lord of the future as of the past.

Strategies for Meeting the Future

That all sounds very well if you say it quickly and don't ask any sticky questions, but just how does one go about being faithful? How does one actually live in hope? What difference does Christian hope make in our lives, in the way in which we face our future?

First, I believe that the Christians, like everyone else, must take some responsibility for figuring out what the future may bring. We need to learn to look at the facts. We need to inspect what data we have available to show us what is likely to happen tomorrow, on the basis of what seems to be true today. There is some good sense in analyzing what present trends indicate. But at the same time, we have to crank into our calculations what present trends do not indicate. After all, most of the significant issues of our time were omitted from consideration when the last generation projected present trends into the future.

Second, and more important, we need to learn to use our imagination to discover the possibility of alternative futures. It's a game, to be sure, but it's the most important game we may ever play. Technologists have a great capacity for sustained clear and precise thinking, but they sometimes are a little short on imagination. Their view of the future usually turns out to be a bigger and better version of the present. What men of hope can contribute is the wild speculation, the fresh impulse, the pipe dream, the far-out trip. We need to ask, "What else might be made to happen? What else can we dare to hope for? What sort of a future do we want, for ourselves and for our children?"

Then we need to face realistically the price we will have to pay in order to make the future we want come true. In this world, you usually have to give something in order to get something. If we want safety, we may have to give up some freedom. If we want freedom, we may have to accept some risks. If we want justice, we may have to give up some of our own advantages. If we want peace, we may have to give up any possibility of influencing the world outside our immediate neighborhood. If we want clean air and water, we may have to give up our automobiles, live in colder houses, and consume fewer goods. Any responsible thinking about the future has to be willing to count the costs.

Finally, and most important, we need to figure out just what demands our future makes on us—now. What can we do to make our future what we want it to be? If we are called to shape our future, we need to begin right now to get things moving. We need to move from thinking to acting, for thought alone does not change history.

Hope differs from optimism because it recognizes that things could go either way. We have no guarantee of a bright and happy future. We have no guarantee of a future at all. We could lose the whole ball game.

But hope differs from pessimism on the same ground. We are not necessarily doomed to failure. We *can* make it. Man *may* prevail. The future is still open and full of possibility. As long as we keep our vision, our resourcefulness, and our will to persevere, we can make a difference. We are called to be actors, to pursue our vision aggressively. That's what it means to be a responsible person. We act in the conviction that if we do our part, God will do his part, and while the result may not be exactly what our blueprints call for, it will not be doomsday either.

From this survey of American values and the themes in our history, we can draw the conclusion that our heritage still lives, still nourishes us and affords us hope. While we cannot claim that Christians have any special insight into our cultural situation, or any special moral standing, still we have a responsible part to play in the future of the nation. And if we have one single contribution to make, it is the hope that looks for God to meet us in history, in the mystery of his grace that sustains and renews us on our way to the future.

SUGGESTED READINGS

The early growth of the doctrine of progress is traced in Arthur A. Ekirch, Jr., *The Idea of Progress in America, 1815–1860* (New York: Columbia University Press, 1944). The beginnings of our loss of confidence and the turn toward psychological-spiritual nostrums are catalogued in Donald Meyer, *The Positive Thinkers* (Garden City, N.Y.: Doubleday, 1965). Joseph Wood Krutch heralded the coming of this century's profound pessimism in *The Modern Temper* (New York: Harcourt, Brace & World, 1956), originally published in the fateful year of 1929. American writers are once again speculating about our future. Their prognostications range from the bleak outlook of Philip E. Slater, *The Pursuit of Loneliness* (Boston: Beacon Press, 1970), through the modest optimism of Theodore A. Roszak, *The Making of a Counter-Culture* (Garden City, N.Y.: Doubleday, 1969), to the almost unqualified (naïve?) optimism of Charles Reich, *The Greening of America* (New York: Random House, 1970; paperback: Bantam, 1971). For a theologically grounded view of the future by a Catholic writer, see Andrew M. Greeley, *A Future to Hope In* (Garden City, N.Y.: Doubleday, 1969). Protestant scholar Martin E. Marty offers a similar view in *The Search for a Useable Future* (New York: Harper & Row, 1969). Both writers approach the future from the perspective of Christian hope.

Session Plans

for group use of
The Future of the American Past

Purpose of the Course

This course is designed to provide an opportunity for concerned Christian lay men and women to engage in meaningful
conversation about the basic values and symbols of American
culture.

If the course stimulates people to think about significant issues,
makes clear to them that there are no easy answers to these very
profound questions, and emboldens them to move into their own
future with courage and hope, it will have been a success. If we
can learn how to relate our Christian heritage to the opportunities and dilemmas of our national life, we will have achieved
a significant goal in Christian education.

Outline of the Course

These sessions are organized around historical themes and cultural values, rather than around issues or problems. The suggested sequence of the six sessions, while somewhat arbitrary,
does have a logical basis.

- After a preliminary "get your feet wet" meeting, the
  first session raises the question of how religious faith
  relates to our cultural heritage. This issue underlies all
  the subsequent discussions.
- The second and third sessions deal with the symbols
  of meaning in our national history. Session Two

focuses on the theme of pilgrimage and asks what
kind of pilgrims we most need for the years ahead. In
Session Three, we explore America's role in the world
and our own attitudes toward that role.

- In Sessions Four and Five, we look at the two fundamental American values of freedom and equality, as-
sessing their present status and our personal attitudes
toward them.

- The final session looks at the future in the context of
the Christian hope and ways by which we can enter
into that future so as to shape it according to our own
values.

The discussion moves from broad historical themes, to personal values, to a call for commitment to action.

Requirements for Participants

No specialized knowledge of American history or expertise in
the heritage of the church is required to participate. The six
chapters provide enough material to initiate discussion and to
provoke debate. Each chapter ends with additional reading suggestions. Though the content of the chapters is not introduced
directly into the design of the sessions, each participant is expected to read the appropriate chapter carefully *before* each
group meeting. This will help set the tone and context for the
discussion. The content of the chapters and the session designs
should structure the experience into more than a freewheeling
bull session.

How to Use the Program

This study course can be used in a number of ways:

- As a parish-wide program for a special season such as
Advent or Lent
- In a small mid-week study group

- In a Sunday-morning adult-education class (though the short time span would necessitate revision of the design)
- In summer conferences for youths and/or adults
- As part of a program to help young people see the relation between their religious heritage and the affairs of the nation

Six sessions will be needed to do justice to the program, and an additional introductory meeting would be ideal. In the get-acquainted session you can distribute materials, rehearse the broad outline and goals of the program, and let participants begin to articulate their feelings about our national tradition.

Fifty minutes is the absolute minimum block of time for each session. One and one-half hours would be optimal, and two hours is not too long if the schedule permits and the coffee holds out. If evening sessions are impossible, and the program is to be held on Sunday mornings, plan to spend two sessions on each topic, taking twelve weeks for the course instead of six.

Resources

The chapters in this book provide background material, but discussion should be keyed to the foreground—that is, where people are. Encourage participants to read the book, but do not let the sessions become merely occasions for hashing over points from their reading. Debate over issues raised by the book may dominate some sessions, while in other sessions the book may not be mentioned at all. Get books into the hands of participants before the course begins. Ask them to read the appropriate chapter before each session.

The July 1973 special issue of *The Anglican Theological Review* mentioned in the Introduction should be available to participants for reference purposes. It can be obtained by writing to:

> The Anglican Theological Review
> 600 Haven Street
> Evanston, Illinois 60201

Spend some time looking through the lists of suggested readings that appear at the end of each chapter. Identify works that seem likely to be of particular interest to your group. If possible, order some for the church library, or at least scout the local libraries and bookstores so that you can let people know where they can locate books that interest them.

Our religious heritage is rich in statements about freedom, equality, mission, and political authority—the things you will be talking about in this course. You may want to refer to biblical passages, hymns, or familiar prayers for the nation that speak to the theme of a particular session.

Encourage participants to introduce issues for discussion as they occur in private or public life. The daily paper will no doubt be reporting the latest crisis; so will radio and TV news broadcasts. TV specials are a particularly rich source of materials. Keep an eye out for relevant plays and movies as they come to your area. Don't worry if such materials upset the schedule of the course. A major public event, or crisis, or controversy may provide the most significant educational experience of the course.

Operation of the Course

Whether the course is given as a parish program involving large numbers of people or as a study-group experience involving only a handful, discussion should take place in a group of ten to fifteen members.

A larger group should be broken down into smaller groups, each one under the leadership of someone selected and trained for the purpose. One person with some educational skill should be given responsibility for overall planning. That person should identify an appropriate number of group leaders to work with the small groups. If enough volunteers are available, two leaders could be assigned to each group, one to serve as discussion leader, the other as observer.

The program director should meet regularly with the leaders of the small groups. Together they should run through the design for each session just as they will do it in each small group. Allow opportunity for a critique of the design so that modifications can be made in accordance with the needs of the groups.

Few special materials are needed for the course. An inviting room with comfortable chairs will facilitate relaxed discussion and interaction. It may be helpful to use participants' homes for the small groups. If classrooms are used, a blackboard may be available. Otherwise, an easel with newsprint and markers will be needed. At evening sessions, coffee or tea helps to set the right tone, so long as refreshments do not get in the way of disciplined discourse.

PRELIMINARY SESSION

Though the course is designed to run for six sessions, a preliminary session is useful for both practical and educational reasons. Books can be distributed, course plans discussed, and participants introduced to each other. Introductions can be used to help people to get into the subject matter of the course.

PURPOSES

To introduce participants to each other
To acquaint them with course materials
To initiate discussion of issues

PROCEDURE

1. Arrange chairs in a circle or other configuration that will encourage face-to-face interchange.

2. As people come in, ask their names, give them name tags, and seat them in the circle.

3. Going around the circle, give each person an opportunity to introduce himself or herself. Suggest that each person take a minute or two for one of the following:

    a. "Tell about your earliest memory of a patriotic feeling. What were the circumstances?"

b. "Tell what makes you most proud to be an American. What is there about America that needs criticism most?"

4. Allow ten to twenty minutes for the group to discuss their experiences. Summarize by pointing out how our personal experience of "my country" varies from individual to individual. Note how any one person's feelings about his country can range from pride and approval to shame and criticism, depending upon what he or she is considering.

5. Explain how the course will operate: the time schedule, relationship between readings and class sessions, need for personal participation, etc. Answer any questions and receive suggestions from the group.

6. Pass out books, note the chapter topics, and assign the reading of chapter 1 for the next session.

SESSION ONE

PURPOSE

To identify some of the ways in which religious norms and values interact with cultural norms and values.

PROCEDURE

1. If there has been no preliminary session, take time to introduce participants to each other. If two-hour sessions have been scheduled, it will be possible to include step 3 of the preliminary session without overburdening the agenda. If a shorter session is planned, a simple exchange of names will have to suffice.

If there has been a preliminary session, proceed directly to:
2. Introduce the following case study:

It has just been announced that the local high school will play its traditional Thanksgiving Day football game against its chief rival on Thanksgiving morning, rather than on the previous evening, as had been the case for the past several years.

You are the members of the local ministerial association, representing the churches of your town. You have regularly held a community-wide ecumenical Thanksgiving Day worship service on that morning. Both you as ministers and your congregations have felt that this service has done much to weld together the religious community of your town. You have now met to decide what to do in the face of this recent decision.

3. Assign up to half the group (but not more than six people) to role-play the ministerial meeting. Assign each of the other group members the task of watching one of the participants in the role play.

4. Allow the role play to continue as long as ten minutes, giving various viewpoints a chance to emerge. Be sure to cut it off, however, before the group makes a decision.

5. Ask nonparticipants to identify the issues as they saw them emerge. List the issues on the blackboard or newsprint.

6. Discuss the proposed solutions in relation to Niebuhr's typology. Which players represent which views of Christ and culture? Which views, if any, have been left out? Why might this be so?

7. Encourage players and observers to identify their own stand on the issue involved in the role play. Does this stand represent a characteristic Christ/culture response?

SUMMARY

Show how positions on this issue illustrate more fundamental differences over the proper relationship of religion and culture. Note the legitimacy of differing viewpoints and the way they may shift from issue to issue.

Questions for further discussion or reflection:

How does our view of the relation of religion to culture affect our views on the following controversial issues?

>   Compulsory military service
>   Abortion laws
>   Prayers in the public schools
>   Corruption in politics

SESSION TWO

The materials for Session One highlighted the fact that our commitments as Americans and our commitments as Christians sometimes intersect and sometimes collide. Session Two analyzes the theme of pilgrimage in our history, both religious and secular, by asking what kinds of people are now needed to keep the sense of pilgrimage alive for the future.

PURPOSE

To identify the kinds of people we regard as important for our pilgrimage into the future.

PROCEDURE

1. Get people seated, wearing name tags, if that seems useful. Pass out pencils and sheets of paper.

2. Have each participant write on the paper without disclosing their choices to others:

   a. The names of three living Americans who come to mind as people you particularly admire (culture heroes)

   b. One or two qualities that you associate with each person, i.e., what makes him or her admirable

   c. Arrange the names in order of priority—most admirable at the top

3. Let each member of the group identify his or her first choice and the reason for it. On the blackboard or newsprint, list each

name and the reason it was introduced. (Use second choices if someone's first choice has already been mentioned.)

4. When the list is complete, discusss the contributions of the various people named. Have the group identify the characteristics they regard as most important for the future.

5. Note which of the valued characteristics are abundant and which seem to be in short supply.

6. Discuss: As we look ahead for the next twenty-five years, what characteristics most need to be nurtured, encouraged, supported? What does this imply for the creation of national leadership? How can we nurture the qualities we find most important? (Remember that national leadership does not mean only political leadership at the federal level. It takes more than politicians to constitute a society.)

SUMMARY

Relate the group's assessment of future needs to the idea of a pilgrim people. Note which of the valued qualities seem appropriate to the pilgrim.

Questions for discussion:

In what sense can Americans today be described as a pilgrim people?

If we are a pilgrim people, what seems to be our intended goal?

SESSION THREE

The theme of pilgrimage suggests a people who see themselves as on the move to a different place. The theme of mission suggests that those people share a common task in the world. A sense of mission has been a persistent feature of the American past, but it is under fire today, partly because people have different ideas of the meaning of mission in our history. Session Three will examine some of these meanings and will help participants to assess their own attitudes toward the idea.

PURPOSE

To clarify the meaning of the concept of American mission and to define our attitude toward it.

PROCEDURE

This session is designed as an exercise in value clarification. It should help people to recognize their own concept of mission and to express it in concrete terms.

1. Read the following statements and ask people to vote their agreement or disagreement with each one. Tally the total responses ("Agree ——, Disagree ——") on the blackboard or newsprint. Do not let people discuss, debate, or qualify their responses. Do it fast.

- a. Most of America's interventions in world affairs have been based on enlightened self-interest.
- b. America's international role is to make the world safe for democracy.
- c. What's good for General Motors is good for the country and vice versa.
- d. The United States should speak softly and carry a big stick.
- e. America's role is to rid the world of communism.
- f. The destiny of America is controlled by a military-industrial complex.
- g. The health of our country depends on respect for our leaders.
- h. America's role in the world is to make the world safe for American business.
- i. The rights of the individual depend upon his freedom to protest against what he does not approve.
- j. Principles of personal morality apply with equal force in international affairs.
- k. America should give of its abundance to underdeveloped areas of the world, even if it hurts.
- l. International politics are essentially amoral.

2. When the voting has been completed, go over the results to identify the degree of consensus within the group. Statements on which all but one or two group members agree can be described as part of the group consensus.

3. Identify those areas on which there is the most significant disagreement; fifty-fifty splits or sixty-forty divisions would fall into this category.

4. Write on the blackboard or newsprint the following sets of polarities—one name on the far left side, the other on the right, with a line connecting the two. Read the description of each character who represents the extreme. Invite each participant to step up to the board and make a mark on each line to identify where he or she stands with respect to the extremes. Read off the description for each character. (Note: If the blackboard or newsprint can be prepared in advance, the description can be written under each name. This would save time.)

Ostrich Oswald————————————————**Gunboat Gary**

America should keep to itself.

America should enforce the peace—with force if necessary.

Bird-Watching Bertha————————————— **Polluting Paul**

We need to clean up our environment even if it means: higher prices, shortages, and changes in the way we live.

We cannot interfere with the manufacturer's right to control his business and make a profit.

Moonstruck Martin————————————— **Bleeding-Heart Bernie**

We should follow up our moon explorations and exploit them in the national interest.

We should rebuild our cities before exploring outer space.

Missionary Mary—————————————**Relativist Roy**

The essence of being Christian is to convert the world to Christ.

We have no right to interfere with others' religions.

Peace-Corps Polly—————————————**Stay-at-Home Stanley**

We should share the benefits of freedom, self-government, and modern living with the exploited peoples of the world.

We should keep to ourselves and allow others to run their own affairs.

5. When all participants have had the opportunity to identify their stands, mark out those areas that seem to represent consensus and those that represent deep divergencies.

6. Using the results of steps 2 and 5, discuss: What perceptions and values do we seem to share, regarding the American mission? What would it mean if the entire country agreed with us?

SUMMARY

Describe the concept of American mission that seemed to arise from the group. Relate the group's concept to the various concepts discussed in the book.

Questions for further discussion:

What does our concept of mission imply for our views on the following issues?

> Defense spending
> Foreign aid
> The mission of the church overseas
> Our system of alliances

What about the differences we have uncovered? Do they damage our sense of unity? Can we live with the differences? Do we need to discuss our differences further so that we can better understand each other? Or would further discussion exacerbate the differences?

SESSION FOUR

Pilgrimage and mission represent ideas about our corporate sense of historical destiny. Turning from these broad and general concepts, Sessions Four and Five begin to consider some of the more intimate personal values especially treasured by most Americans. Freedom means different things to different people. Session Four raises the question of what freedoms we most value for ourselves.

PURPOSES

To make the concept of freedom concrete and particular. To help people identify those areas in which freedom is most important to them.

PROCEDURE

1. Break the group down into pairs to work on the first part of the exercise.

2. Ask each pair, working together, to list ten ways in which freedom is threatened or restricted.

3. When the lists have been completed, ask each pair to select their three top-priority items, arranging them in order of importance.

4. Have each pair share their results with the whole group. Write each item on the blackboard or newsprint, noting duplications.

5. Discuss: What freedoms do we most want to see guaranteed for ourselves and for our children in the future?

6. For each major item, have the group identify the forces that tend to make for achievement of that particular freedom and the forces tending to inhibit it.

SUMMARY

Interpret the data produced by the group to show the freedoms most valued, the freedoms most endangered, and the group consensus on what chances freedom has in the future.

Questions for further discussion:

In our discussion, what freedoms—or threats to freedom—have we overlooked, though they may be of major importance to people other than ourselves?

How can we distinguish limitations placed on freedom by the need for order and/or discipline from the limitations that constitute repression?

SESSION FIVE

Freedom and equality are seen as contradictory concepts in many societies, but in the minds of Americans, they go together. Like freedom, equality can have many meanings. This session will explore some implications of the idea of equality, giving participants an opportunity to register their commitment to equality as they perceive it.

PURPOSE

To pose the issue of uniformity versus diversity as it relates to equality; to enable participants to clarify their own commitment to the value of equality.

PROCEDURE

1. Introduce the following case history for discussion:

You are an American Indian, the father of an eleven-year-old boy who is attending government school on your reservation. Your tribe lives in poverty and squalor, and you harbor few hopes for the future. Your son has just been offered a full scholarship to attend a leading private boarding school in New England. The grant will cover tuition, room, and board for his entire school career. You are trying to make up your mind what to do.

    a. What factors might lead you to decide to accept the scholarship for your son?
    b. What factors might lead you to reject it?
    c. What might be some possible outcomes, both for good and for evil, if you accept the scholarship? If you reject it?
(Note: This is the father's choice. Don't cop out by saying that we should leave it up to the son.)

2. List the following statements in the blackboard or newsprint (preferably before the session begins). They represent polar positions, so they should be spaced at the far sides of the

paper. Connect the two extremes with a line. Invite participants to make their mark on the line where their view on the matter places them.

☐_____☐

Gifted children should receive first priority for special consideration by our public schools.

Children with learning disabilities should receive first claim on our scarce educational resources.

☐_____☐

Decisions about public policy are best made by experts, who know the most about the subject.

Decisions about public policy are best made by the people most affected by them.

☐_____☐

Candidates for public office should be people of special qualifications who have demonstrated a high level of professional competence.

Candidates for public office should be ordinary people, close to their constituents and sympathetic to their needs.

☐_____☐

Store and restaurant employees are as good as their customers. They should be treated as equals.

Customers have the right to expect a certain amount of deference from sales persons, waiters, etc.

☐_____☐

Executives, major public officials, professors, and others in leadership positions are entitled to some special privileges, such as private dining facilities, lounges, parking spaces, etc.

Regardless of position, everybody in an organization should be treated alike.

3. When all participants have made their marks, note the spread of opinion, identify those areas in which most people agree and those where disagreement is strong.

4. Discuss those areas that show the most disparity. Ask members with the views closest to the extremes to share with the group the reasons that they placed themselves at the point they did. Give the group enough time so that misunderstandings are clarified, qualifications are offered, and the remaining core of genuine disagreement is identified.

SUMMARY

1. Referring back to the case study, show how it demonstrates the difficulty of achieving equality in the face of the irreconcilable conflict between uniformity and diversity.

2. When you look at where members of the group placed their marks in the above exercise, what would you say about their commitment to the value of equality? Share your perceptions with them and see if they agree or disagree.

Questions for further discussion:

When we opt for a society in which all participate in the same mainstream, what genuine values are likely to get lost?

If we affirm the right of each subgroup in our society to retain its separate identity and cultural heritage, what genuine values are likely to get lost?

If we set out to treat everyone alike, what genuine values are likely to get lost?

If we accept a society based on privilege and prerogative, what genuine values are likely to get lost?

SESSION SIX

We have looked at our past, at the themes that give it meaning and the values that it embodies. We should have a better idea of how the American tradition fares in the present. Having tested

DWIGHT DAVID EISENHOWER, PRESIDENT

Other titles in this series:

FIVE FIRST LADIES:
A Look into the Lives of Nancy Reagan,
Rosalynn Carter, Betty Ford, Pat
Nixon, and Lady Bird Johnson
by Elizabeth S. Smith

JIMMY CARTER, PRESIDENT
by Betsy Covington Smith

**LYNDON BAINES JOHNSON,
PRESIDENT**
by John Devaney

GERALD R. FORD, PRESIDENT
by Sallie K. Randolph

DWIGHT DAVID EISENHOWER, PRESIDENT

By Elizabeth Van Steenwyk

Walker and Company
New York, New York

First published in the United States of America
in 1987 by the Walker Publishing Company, Inc.

Published simultaneously in Canada by John Wiley & Sons
Canada, Limited, Rexdale, Ontario.

Library of Congress Cataloging-in-Publication Data

Van Steenwyk, Elizabeth.
    Dwight David Eisenhower, president.
    Roo562   52817
    (Presidential biography series)
    Bibliography: p.
    Includes index.
    Summary: A biography of the commanding general of the
Allied forces in Europe in World War II who became the
thirty-fourth president of the United States.
    1. Eisenhower, Dwight D. (Dwight David), 1890–1969—
Juvenile literature. 2. Presidents—United States—Biog-
raphy—Juvenile literature. [1. Eisenhower, Dwight D. (Dwight
David), 1890–1969. 2. Presidents]
    I. Title. II. Series.

JuV   E836.V34   1987   973.921'092'4   [B]   [92]   86-26730
    ISBN 0-8027-6670-6
    ISBN 0-8027-6671-4 (lib. bdg.)

Book Design by Ellen Pugatch

Printed in the United States of America

10 9 8 7 6 5 4 3 2 1

Contents

ACKNOWLEDGMENTS

Special thanks are due Martin M. Teasley, Assistant Director of the Dwight D. Eisenhower Library, and Kathy Struss, a member of the staff, for their help in locating photographs to illustrate this book. Thanks are also due Barbara Simon for her assistance and enthusiasm in the preparation of this manuscript.

Photographic credit: All photographs were furnished by the Dwight D. Eisenhower Library, Abilene, Kansas. Some of these photographs originated with the U.S. Navy, the U.S. Army, National Park Service, Columbia University, Army Signal Corps.

1

Growing Up In Abilene

On Friday morning, January 20, 1961, shortly before noon, Dwight David Eisenhower, 34th president of the United States, rode down Pennsylvania Avenue in Washington, D.C. with John Fitzgerald Kennedy, soon to become the 35th president. The day was crisp and brilliant with sunshine as the oldest man ever to hold the office of president (at that time) accompanied the youngest ever elected to his inauguration at the Capitol building.

Both men heard the cheering of the crowd and responded to it, knowing it was meant for both of them. For President-elect Kennedy, it was the beginning of adulation by the citizenry. But displays of deep affection had followed President Eisenhower for a long time now. For twenty years he had been a leader in war and peace, deeply loved by friends and admired even by enemies.

Now he considered his job finished. After the ceremony, including the prayers, the recitation by the old poet, Robert Frost, and the speech by the new president, Dwight David Eisenhower could slip away with his wife, Mamie, to Gettysburg and their home there. For the first time since he'd left his parents' home in Abilene, Kansas, fifty years before, the president was going to a home of his own, this time to stay.

President Eisenhower had lived in many houses, small and large, simple and elegant, after leaving that two-story frame house on Fourth Street in Abilene. None, perhaps, left as great an impression. His parents had rented it when he was eight, and to young Dwight it had "seemed a mansion, with its upstairs bedrooms."

Nevertheless, the family was packed in tightly, four boys in two double beds jammed into one small bedroom, mother and father and infant son in another, and Grandfather Jacob Eisenhower occupying a small bedroom downstairs.

Grandfather Jacob and his family had arrived in 1878 to establish farms near Abilene, leaving behind rich lands, abundant crops, and a beautiful home in Pennsylvania. Although well-to-do and successful, the Eisenhowers felt they could do even better in Kansas than in Pennsylvania.

And there was more. The frontier of the nation beckoned to the restless itch in nineteenth-century Americans to move on and settle the West. The Eisenhowers were just as restless as other Americans.

Jacob and his family were thrifty and hard-working in the Pennsylvania Dutch tradition, as all the Eisenhowers had been before. Their ordered, simple life was an extension of their religious beliefs as members of the American Mennonite sect, later known as the Church of the Brethren in Christ.

The sect's beliefs developed strong individual character in its members. They believed in hard work, self-reliance, thriftiness, strictness in their behavior, and they were pacifists. Jacob was a minister of the church as well as a farmer and, therefore, a man of peace. (During World War II, members of the Brethren remained pacifists even as Jacob's grandson became a wartime leader.)

At the time of the Eisenhowers' arrival in 1878, Abilene was still suffering from a reputation as one of the wildest towns in the nation. For awhile after the Civil War, the Kansas-Pacific Railroad stopped at Abilene, making it the journey's end for cattle driven along the Chisholm Trail from Texas. It wasn't unusual for the stockyards to contain one hundred thousand head of cattle waiting to be shipped east.

Abilene had also known its share of gunslingers, saloon keepers, and riffraff that gathered in cow towns to relieve cowboys of their wages. It, too, hosted the heroes behind sheriffs' badges that circled around to protect the innocent and not so innocent. In Abilene's heyday, one of its better-known citizens was Wild Bill Hickock.

Then the railroad laid tracks farther west and the cowboys no longer came to Abilene. Overnight the heroes and villains disappeared and it became a quiet rural town with nothing to distinguish it from thousands of others on the midwest prairie. Nothing much ever happened, and the townspeople valued their peace and friendship and principles. None of the homes had a lock on the door. Abilene became a perfect place to nurture a future hero who would eventually become its best-known citizen.

Jacob and his family found Kansas to be at once harsh and promising. Its climate ranged from dry, dusty summers to bitter, snowbound winters. But the land they chose in the valley of the Smokey Hill River was rich, and their crops were soon abundant and plentiful.

They were successful at once and, after a few years, Jacob established a small bank in the village of Hope, near Abilene. It was not his intention to do anything but farm, however, and he expected his sons to do the same. One son, David, declined and instead chose to attend a church-affiliated college for two years. There he met and married Ida Elizabeth Stover in 1885. She also was a member of the Brethren sect and said to be strong-willed and independent.

The young married couple settled in Hope and started a small store with capital borrowed from Jacob's bank. Three years later the store failed, all the money was lost and, in shame and humiliation, David Eisenhower left Kansas and took a poorly paid railroad job in Denison, Texas.

David and Ida's third child was born there on October 14, 1890. They named him David Dwight, but to avoid confusion with his father, soon switched his name to Dwight David. The following spring, the family moved back to Abilene where David took a job as a mechanic with the Belle Springs Creamery, operated by the Brethren. He made fifty dollars a month, not a large sum with which to support a growing family.

It has been said that David never recovered his self-confidence after the early failure of his store. But Ida brought all her energy and ambition to their situation and determined to make the best of it. Through her personal motivation and religious beliefs, Ida Eisenhower would stamp her six boys with a philosophy of determination and a need to excel, never admitting defeat or showing disappointment.

By the most careful management of their meager funds plus hard work, the David Eisenhowers prevailed. A large barn sat in the middle of their three-acre lot, the family kept a horse, a couple of cows, chickens, and pigs. They also grew their own fruits and vegetables, giving the young boys plenty of work before and after school. Even if cash was short, the family had enough to eat from its garden.

Because David worked at the creamery long hours, six days a week, Ida was in complete charge at home, assigning household chores to her sons and, most of the time, doling out the discipline when necessary. The boys worked inside, helping with the cooking and cleaning, as well as caring for the livestock and garden outdoors. As soon as they were old enough, each worked at the creamery doing odd jobs to bring in extra cash.

Ida rarely resorted to spankings, believing in self-discipline instead, which she preached constantly to the six boys. If serious discipline was needed, David was asked to settle it when he came home from work, usually with a maple switch or a leather strap.

The boys wore hand-me-downs to school, and that meant occasional ridicule from classmates. When Dwight wore his mother's battered old button shoes to elementary school one day, he expected to be jeered at, and was. A fight resulted, and he quickly learned to use his fists.

"It made us scrappers," Dwight's brother, Edgar, said later. "Any time anybody walked on us, they heard from us. It didn't make any difference how big or how little he was, if he did something that infringed on our rights, he got a punch then and there."

Soon the Eisenhower boys had earned a reputation as those tough roughnecks from the wrong side of the railroad tracks. And they adopted the attitude of one-for-all-and-all-for-one, although some of them enjoyed fighting more than the others. In order of

Dwight's fifth grade class at Lincoln School, Abilene. The year is 1900. He is second from left, front row.

age they were: Arthur, Edgar, Dwight, Roy, Paul, who died in infancy, Earl, and Milton.

At different times, each Eisenhower boy answered to "Ike," a nickname their mother hated. For a long time, Edgar was known as "Big Ike" and Dwight as "Little Ike." Another brother was sometimes called "Red Ike" and a fourth "Ugly Ike." When Milton started school, Dwight graduated to "Big Ike" and Milton became "Little Ike." But it was Dwight who kept the nickname throughout adulthood and became better known as Ike than as Dwight.

Ike went to school regularly according to his attendance records, but his preference for outdoor life was no secret. The Smokey Hill River, a few miles south of Abilene, was the scene of many of his activities, including hunting, fishing, camping, and cooking. Because his mother taught him to help her cook at an early age,

Camping on the Smokey Hill River with friends. The year is 1907, Ike is front, center.

Ike's friends always asked him to do the cooking on their camping trips. It would become a lifelong hobby.

Ike tried and participated in all sports, winter and summer, spring and fall. He became such a good football and baseball player that, by the time he reached high school, he was a regular on both teams. In the winter he skated or hooked sleds behind horses for rides around town. He also boxed and fought on the playgrounds any time at all. Because of his short temper, he was never at a loss for opponents.

One fistfight stands out. His opponent, Wesley Merrifield, was labeled the town bully. He was heavier, stronger, and more experienced than thirteen-year-old Ike. A crowd gathered on the vacant lot at Third and Broadway as Ike took him on. Soon Ike seemed beaten; both eyes were swollen closed. But two hours later, when the boys could barely stand, Merrifield said that he couldn't lick the Eisenhower kid, and only then did Ike quit.

The Eisenhower boys got a dose of religion at every meal. Before breakfast their father read passages from the Bible, and after supper they all sat around and read from the Bible again, passing it from hand to hand. "This was a good way to get us to read the Bible mechanically," Milton Eisenhower recalled. "I am not sure it was a good way to help us understand it."

Often their house was used for religious services and their mother played the piano to accompany the singing of hymns. By now, the parents had left the Brethren sect and gone to something even more austere. Later, they would take part in the services of Jehovah's Witnesses.

Probably Ike's closest friend during his growing-up years was his brother, Edgar. They played and worked together, fought one common foe together, and occasionally each other. When Ike developed blood poisoning after skinning his knee at the age of fourteen, it was Edgar to whom he turned for help.

For days Ike lay in his big oak bed and fought the poison that ran through his body. A doctor was called and told Ike's parents the only way to save their son's life was to amputate his leg. But Ike refused to let it happen. He insisted Edgar promise that, if Ike went into a coma, Edgar would prevent the surgery.

For two days the doctor tried to convince David and Ida that amputation was the only way to proceed, while Edgar stood guard outside the bedroom door. Miraculously, Ike recovered, but he had been ill so long and was so weak after his recovery that he had to repeat his first year of high school.

In his class of thirty-one, Ike was above average, excelling in history, his favorite subject, discovering heroes like Hannibal and George Washington. He liked math, too, reflecting his interests in exact, practical knowledge and solutions. Philosophy and other abstract ideas were not for him, so he memorized dates and names of battles and wars and left the worry of why there were wars to others.

When he wasn't studying or participating in sports, Ike worked at many odd jobs to bring money into the household. He delivered newspapers, worked as a harvest hand and, for a time, sandpa-

Ike and Edgar played together on the 1908 Abilene High School baseball team. Ike is second from right in the back row, Edgar in the center of the middle row.

pered wooden horses in the nearby merry-go-round factory. Once he even talked his mother into teaching him how to make hot tamales. Then he made them up in large batches and sold them three for five cents.

By his senior year of high school, Ike had grown to his full adult size of just under six feet and weighed about 150 pounds. But now that he had become a star football player, the school board could no longer finance the team.

The students were unwilling to give up the game, however, and formed an association with Ike as president to raise funds to support the team. They raised enough money to keep the team play-

1908 Abilene High School football team. Ike is third from left, back row.

ing and in uniform, though not always providing transportation to play in neighboring towns.

But Ike proved himself in a crisis. When the team lacked transportation fares to Chapman, twelve miles away, for an important game, Ike led his teammates to the railroad station. There they hopped the freight cars to Chapman, won the game, and returned to Abilene in the same manner.

Although Edgar was two years older than Ike, they graduated from high school together in the class of 1909. According to the class prophet, Edgar was going to become president of the United States and Ike would be a history professor at Yale. Edgar already had decided on a career in law and enrolled at the University of Michigan. Ike decided to work during that year to help pay for Edgar's schooling and he began a full-time job at the creamery, working seven nights a week. They planned that Edgar would later help Ike finance his college education.

With Edgar away at the university, Ike began to go around with a boy named Swede Hazlett. Swede was preparing to take the entrance exams for Annapolis and persuaded Ike to do so, too. Although a military education would be contrary to his parents' religious beliefs, Ike decided to apply, primarily for the free education.

He knew there would be competition, so he began to cram for the tests. He returned to high school, taking classes in chemistry and mathematics after working all night at the creamery. J. W. Howe, who owned the local newspaper, allowed him to use his excellent personal collection of books to study.

In November, Ike went to Topeka for his examination and returned home later, not certain how well he had done. But when the results were posted, he had scored 87.7 percent, the highest grade of all. Soon after, he learned that he was overage to enter Annapolis, since he had reached his twentieth birthday in October.

After checking entrance requirements to West Point and finding there was no age restriction, Ike applied there. In January, 1911, he passed its examination with another high grade. Although his plans to enter did not please his parents, they let him make the choice, allowing his own conscience to guide him. Ida Eisenhower never let her son see the grief she felt when he left home for West Point the following June.

2

West Point and the Future

On June 2, 1911, the Abilene *Daily Reflector* carried the following brief news item:

> Dwight Eisenhower left today for West Point where he will join the freshman class. . . . He is a bright young man and is a good athlete and will make good.

The young man who boarded the Union Pacific Railroad that day in Abilene for the ride east to West Point, New York, was an uncomplicated country boy by contemporary standards. The Abilene school system had taught him the academic basics and his parents had taught him fairness, self-discipline, and the need for hard work and high moral standards.

His life so far, however, had given him a restricted view of the rest of the world. He knew little of the social and economic issues of the day. The growing international unrest that would soon cause World War I was not a part of the Abilene lexicon, and he had only a smattering of knowledge about problems in his own country. Rapid industrialization in the United States was not a concern in the one-industry town of Abilene. Racism wasn't either. Like most people in the Midwest, young Ike felt that the North had done its duty to blacks by freeing them during the Civil War.

But if he lacked understanding or information about the rest of the world outside Abilene, young Dwight knew himself. He knew he was physically strong, mentally sure, and that he had a great capacity for growth. And he wasn't afraid of the future or

Ike stopped in Ann Arbor, Michigan to visit his brother Edgar, on the way to West Point. The year is 1911.

to grow with it. Now, as he rode east, Dwight Eisenhower, nearly twenty-one years old, was ready to handle anything that might come his way.

And it was a good thing, too, because he was about to enter a tough school with a tough system designed to turn individuals into members of a team tougher than any on which they had ever played.

Thomas Jefferson, as president, had signed a bill in 1802 authorizing the establishment of the United States Military Academy at West Point. Gray fortresslike buildings had been erected on the rugged hills overlooking the Hudson River, and the training of young officers inside those walls in the following years had been demanding and relentless. Some of the best young minds attended because it was tuition-free. Its students were appointed by congressmen who selected carefully, and its entrance examinations were rigid. Dwight Eisenhower would have keen competition.

At once he was plunged into the tough, disciplined life, assigned to F Company, traditionally the company of the jocks. The entering cadets—called "plebes"—were treated as if they were specks of dirt. Ike remembered that the first thing plebes learned was that they were "awkward, clumsy, and of unequaled stupidity." They were made to stand stiffly at attention by the older cadets, asked unanswerable questions, insulted, shouted at, and then ordered to do fifty or a hundred pushups for a minor infraction of a miniscule rule.

They marched everywhere in formation—to meals, to classes, to dormitories, to chapel, to athletic activities, and even to extra work. Everything was accomplished in double time by everyone, or they didn't stay very long.

And plebes did leave. Some couldn't take the humiliation, the lack of freedom, or the academic competition. But Ike seemed better prepared in many ways than his classmates. He was older than many in the freshman class, he was in great physical shape, and he could see the point to the hazing and laugh at it.

Ike's sense of humor came in handy once when he and another plebe were caught in a minor mistake. They were ordered by an upperclassman to report to his room at the end of the day in "full-dress coats," which meant complete uniform. Ike and the other plebe decided to have some fun of their own, and took the order literally. When the time came for them to appear in the upperclassman's room, they arrived wearing the full-dress coats, but nothing else. This joke had been pulled before by other cadets, including Edgar Allan Poe when he was a cadet before the Civil War. And now it got the desired effect, too. Other cadets came in and laughed, not at Ike and his friend, but at the upperclassman. Of course, they later had to stand extra hazing from the cadet on whom they'd played the joke, but to their minds it was well worth it.

Ike's sense of fair play, however, prevented him from becoming a true hazer when he became an upperclassman. An experience in his sophomore year cured him. After hazing a plebe, he told a roommate, "I've just done something that was stupid and unforgivable. I managed to make a man ashamed of the work he did to earn a living." Ike never hazed another plebe.

He had come to the Point not to haze, nor obey orders, but to get an education and play football. Now he concentrated on both. During his freshman year he played football and baseball, though realizing he was too light and not fast enough for the varsity teams. In his second year, his goal was to gain weight and work on speed and hitting.

During the summer he ate everything and worked tirelessly on the track. When the 1912 season began, he weighed 174 pounds, had gained quickness, and he tackled every appropriate person on the football field. After his first few games, the newspapers began to talk of him as a possible All-American.

During a midseason game against Tufts, Ike was injured and had to be carried from the field with a rapidly swelling knee. After a couple of weeks in the hospital, the swelling went down and he returned to a normal schedule.

A few days later, he was performing a riding trick called "monkey drill," leaping on and off his galloping horse. His injured knee was reinjured, this time tearing tendons and cartilage, and he spent

Football practice at West Point. 1912.

the next month in the hospital. His athletic career had ended. He favored the knee for the rest of his life and was never again able to run at full speed.

He considered quitting, and only the thought of getting a free education kept him at the Academy. He later wrote that the "end of my career as an active football player had a profound effect on me." Only after he was asked to help coach some of the plebes and scrubs did his depression lift. He became an excellent coach during his years at the Point, and later he coached many football teams at the various posts to which he was assigned.

Although half the reason for his being at West Point was gone, Ike did not let the crisis ruin his life there. Finally he ignored it and moved on, going to class, having fun, and getting more demerits along the way.

In an official report, an officer said, "We saw in Eisenhower a not uncommon type, a man who would thoroughly enjoy his army life, giving both to duty and recreation their fair values, but we did not see in him a man who would throw himself into a job so completely that nothing else would matter."

No one predicted he would become a general, although he did make cadet corporal once. But he was well-liked by his classmates and participated in many extracurricular activities that made him well-known on campus. One of his close friends was Omar Bradley, and of him Ike predicted that "some of us will someday be bragging that 'Sure, General Bradley was a classmate of mine.' "

Ike did well enough to rank 61st academically in his class of 164 men at graduation time. In conduct, he ranked 95th. Just before graduation, however, he was told that, because of his bad knee, he would not be commissioned. Undisturbed, Ike merely shrugged at this latest misfortune. Apparently he didn't want to be a soldier that much. Instead, he decided to go to Argentina because he had been interested in that country for a number of years and thought he might try his luck down there.

Then the army doctor changed his mind and said that Ike could have his commission after all, providing he stayed in the infantry. The cavalry was no place for a man with a knee like his.

West Point graduation portrait. 1915.

Before graduation, each cadet was asked to list his preference for first duty assignment. This was 1915, and the war in Europe had become more personal to Americans with the sinking of the ship, the *Lusitania*, by a German U-boat. It was expected that most cadets would request duty nearest the action.

Not so with Cadet Eisenhower. For a reason that is not clear to historians, he chose the Philippines for first posting and felt so confident he would be sent there that he ordered only tropical uniforms.

So, on June 12, 1915, he graduated as Second Lieutenant Dwight David Eisenhower, U.S. Army, Infantry, an officer and a gentleman. Shortly thereafter, he was sent on his first tour of duty—to the Nineteenth Infantry Regiment at Fort Sam Houston near San Antonio, Texas. He couldn't have known that President Woodrow Wilson had decided not to station American troops around the world because of the European war.

He arrived in Texas in debt because he had to buy a complete new set of uniforms, olive drabs for garrison duty and blues for dress. When he was offered $150 to coach a football team at nearby Peacock Military Academy, it must have seemed like fate stepping in to lend a hand.

Fort Sam Houston was considered good duty for young officers. It was a lively place and the center of social activities for the military. Many officers retired nearby, buying ranches yet maintaining ties with the active army and establishing military academies for the schooling of their young sons.

The Fort also attracted a number of wealthy families who wintered in San Antonio and, as a result, young, single women were usually available for the eligible young officers to date.

One of these families, the Douds, came each year from Denver, Colorado, bringing with them three lively daughters, the eldest of whom was Marie Geneva Doud, whose nickname was Mamie. In 1915, she was eighteen, slender, and gregarious. Her brown hair was combed to fall in a wave over her rather high forehead.

· John Sheldon Doud, her father, had retired after making a small fortune from the packing house business in Iowa. Her mother was called Min by everyone and was as lively and full of fun as her daughters.

One October Sunday afternoon, a month after he'd arrived in San Antonio, Lieutenant Eisenhower was serving as officer of the day, walking the post on an inspection tour. As he recalled it in his memoirs, *At Ease*, Mrs. Harris, the wife of a major in the Nineteenth Infantry, was standing in a group of visitors and called to him, "Ike, won't you come over here? I have some people I'd like you to meet."

"Sorry," he called back. "I'm on guard and have to stand an inspection tour."

July 1, 1916. Denver, Colorado. Lieutenant and Mrs. Eisenhower's wedding portrait.

"We didn't ask you to come over to stay," Mrs. Harris called out. "Just come over and meet these friends of mine."

He walked across the street and met the Douds, but he had eyes only for Mamie. She was, in his words, "saucy in the look about her face and in her whole attitude." When he asked her if she would help him finish walking his rounds, she agreed.

Ike had fallen in love, but he was only one of many boyfriends for Mamie. He called her the next day to ask for a date, but she told him she was busy for the next month. Finally, he asked her for a date one month in advance and she accepted. Gradually, he eliminated the competition for Mamie's time and attention and on Valentine's Day, 1916, he proposed and she accepted. He gave her his class ring and they planned to marry in November.

Meantime, Ike had applied for a transfer to the aviation section of the army simply because he was bored with the routine of being in the infantry. He was soon accepted and hurried over to the Douds to share the exciting news.

But the Douds found the news less than exciting. They found it to be an irresponsible act by their daughter's new fiancé. Mr. Doud told Ike that if he wanted to get into such a risky business as flying, the wedding would have to be called off.

Ike thought it over, weighing his new career against marriage to Mamie. Finally he made his decision and withdrew his application to the new aviation section of the army.

But now Mamie had some demands of her own. The escalating war in Europe had made her nervous that Ike might be sent overseas before their marriage occurred in November. She insisted that it take place earlier, so they were married on July 1, 1916, in Denver. The bridegroom, wearing a white uniform he had purchased for his expected duty in the Philippines, was promoted to first lieutenant on the same day.

3

Another Reason to Excel

Ike and Mamie spent their short honeymoon in Abilene as none of the Eisenhower family had attended the wedding. Mamie said that she was especially pleased to have so many brothers now, after having had none for her first nineteen years. But it was Ida and Mamie who became friends instantly.

There is only one recorded complaint that Mrs. Eisenhower ever made known about her new daughter-in-law. Mamie always referred to her husband as Ike, a nickname that the older woman disliked. When Mamie wrote once to tell about a trip she and Ike enjoyed, Mrs. Eisenhower replied by letter, "I am very glad [about the trip], but who is this Ike you are traveling with?"

Now Ike and Mamie returned to sweltering Fort Sam Houston in mid-July, 1916, and moved into his old bachelor quarters to begin married life.

His parents had emphasized a need to excel as he grew up, and Ike had pursued that goal thus far. Probably it was due to his parents' urging as much as his own. But now Lieutenant Eisenhower was a married man. His wife was accustomed to the finer things of life—maids, big houses, and money for luxuries. It would be difficult for her to adjust to a first lieutenant's pay and housing of two rooms and a bath. He needed to work hard, move up in rank—quickly.

The war in Europe had been raging since 1914. Beginning in January, 1917, the Germans renewed their attack on neutral American ships in the Atlantic Ocean. President Wilson began to increase the size of the U.S. Army as a way of preparing for a

war that was sure to come. Now Eisenhower found himself assigned to a recruiting camp about twenty miles from Fort Sam
Houston and Mamie. When war was declared the following April,
he made constant applications to be transferred to a combat unit.
Instead, he was sent to Georgia to become a staff officer at a
training camp. He was a captain now and filled his job well, taking
recruits into the field and preparing them for trench warfare.

Two months later he was ordered to duty at Fort Leavenworth,
Kansas, to train new second lieutenants. Again and again he ap-
plied for combat duty until he was officially reprimanded by the
War Department for the repeated requests. Angry and resentful,
Eisenhower thought of resigning when the war was over.

Then he received orders to go to Camp Meade, Maryland, to
join a newly formed tank battalion. His mood changed. Tanks
were the new weapon and were in use on the front. Surely now
he would see active duty. When orders came for the battalion to
sail for France and he was to go with it, Eisenhower went to New
York to oversee every detail of the embarkation and voyage.

Back at Camp Meade, however, he learned the army had other
plans for him. Because he had shown such exceptional organiza-
tional ability, he was placed in charge of the brand-new Tank
Corps to be organized and trained at Camp Colt near Gettysburg,
Pennsylvania.

"My mood was black," Eisenhower would recall about that
transfer years later.

There was a bright side to his transfer. Mamie had just had
their first child, a baby boy named Doud Dwight, whom they
nicknamed "Icky." Now she and the baby joined him, renting a
small house in Gettysburg. Ike was very proud of his son and
showed him much love and affection. He was a warmhearted man
and appreciated this time spent with his little family, knowing
that professional soldiers often have to spend long periods away
from them.

Meanwhile, his job could have become a disaster. When he
took charge at the beginning of March, Major (temporary rank)
Eisenhower found a camp that had swollen rapidly to ten thousand

men and six hundred officers. The men were hungry because rations hadn't arrived, and they were freezing in icy tents without stoves or cots.

The situation could have gotten out of hand. But Eisenhower ordered campfires built and sent officers out to buy food as well as straw from neighboring farmers. As a country boy, he knew that straw would be warmer than cots to sleep on.

In addition, no training procedures existed. No tanks did either. Immediately he established "theoretical tank training," giving the men instructions on how tanks were constructed, operated, and maneuvered. Then he instituted field training, using boxes for tanks. To the untrained eye, this might have seemed ludicrous, yet Ike's men needed only a little additional training when they climbed into real tanks in France.

The camp became a model of military efficiency and precision under his direction, and he soon was promoted to lieutenant colonel, again temporary rank.

Finally orders came for Ike to go to France. He was ordered to move the entire Tank Corps but, by the time he arrived in New York for embarkation, the Armistice had been signed.

Again he considered resigning, but when he was transferred back to Camp Meade to continue his work with tanks, he decided to stay. He was convinced that tanks were the weapons of the future, and he looked around to find other officers who agreed with him.

One of these officers was Colonel George S. Patton, Jr., who had seen action in France. The two men, though different in background, personality, and approach to life, immediately became fast friends and constant companions. They complemented each other and learned from each other. They made a good team.

During his first year at Meade, Ike lived in bachelor quarters as there was little or no housing for families. Then, in 1920, some barracks were turned into family units and that spring Mamie and Icky joined Ike. Now the Patton and Eisenhower families met socially and, through the Pattons, Ike met a senior officer who changed the direction of his career.

Major Eisenhower at the Tank Center, Camp Meade, Maryland. 1919.

Brigadier General Fox Connor was an officer of exceptional reputation and influence. He spoke excellent French, was widely read, and was considered a real brain in the army. Privately wealthy and married to an heiress, he also had style. In addition, he was a philosopher and a student of military history. He was a good man for Ike to know.

Otherwise, 1920 was not a good year for the Eisenhowers. Congress cut back the size of the army, and Ike found his permanent rank reduced to major. Then he was rejected for special training at the Infantry School, which would have led to the Command and General Staff School. It is here that command officers are developed for field leadership of the entire army. Ike was beginning to wonder: Had he reached the limit of his military career?

Toward the end of the year, a far worse event happened. Little Icky, now three years old, developed scarlet fever. Although the camp doctor did everything possible for the little boy, including calling in specialists and sending the child to the hospital, he died in his father's arms shortly after New Year's.

For months, as Ike later said, he was "on the ragged edge of a breakdown" from sorrow. The young couple was inconsolable and drifted through their days without interest or direction.

Meantime, General Connor had been transferred to the Panama Canal Zone and he asked Ike if he would like to come along as his executive officer. Twice Ike's request for transfer was turned down, until late in the year his orders finally were approved. Ike and Mamie arrived in Panama early in January, 1922, relieved to be gone from Camp Meade and the sorrow of a year ago.

In addition to all the other things that he could do, General Connor was a natural teacher. Now he had a pupil who was eager to learn. Before long, Ike's studies included not only military history but philosophy and English literature as well.

The two men often had to ride horseback from one outpost to another in the Canal Zone. At night, after they made camp, they sat by the fire discussing the Civil War, or Napoleon or Hannibal's strategies, or the writings of Earl von Clausewitz and Ferdinand

Foch. Their talks covered more than military history and philosophy, however. They talked about the present as well as the future army. Connor predicted another war, greater than the one just past. He said the key to victory would be persuading the United States and its allies to work together. He also told Ike to "always take your job seriously, never yourself," an adage that Eisenhower would repeat again and again.

Years later, after President Eisenhower retired and spoke of the great leaders with whom he had worked, he said, "Fox Connor was the ablest man I ever knew."

In the summer of 1922, Mamie went home to Denver to await the arrival of their second child. Ike was given leave to be with her when John Sheldon Doud was born in August.

When Ike's two-year tour at the Canal Zone was finished, he carried out short assignments in Colorado and Georgia. Part of this time he coached another football team as he felt his career direction drifting again. Meanwhile, General Connor was using his influence to get Ike an assignment to the Command and General Staff College in Fort Leavenworth, Kansas.

Ike knew the assignment was crucial to his future, yet on the day he was accepted, he was terrified, remembering his less than brilliant performance at West Point. He decided to prepare for this opportunity made possible by General Connor and approached what he later termed "a watershed in my life" with a great deal of preparation, studying for months before his classes actually started.

When his course of study began in August, 1925, Ike stepped up his pace. He attended classes or read all day. At night he studied in a quiet room in his house, often with an old friend from Fort Sam Houston days, Leonard Gerow. Mamie recalled that year as one in which she never saw her husband.

Competition was keen; some officers dropped out and it was rumored that there was more than one suicide. But Ike needed to excel and now he did, graduating in June, 1926, first in a class of 275 superior officers. His name was beginning to be known as someone to watch.

Eisenhower family portrait taken in 1925 shortly before Major Eisenhower began Command and General Staff College. *(L to R) Roy; Arthur
and Earl on swing; standing, Edgar; seated, David, the father; standing,
Milton; then Ida. Seated in front, Dwight David (Ike).*

The reward for excellence was not long in coming when Ike
was assigned to the Battle Monuments Commission in Washington, D.C. General John J. Pershing, the general who had commanded Americans in World War I and now was chief of staff,
had long wanted someone to write a guide to the World War I
battlefields in France. Ike became that man and began to study
the "war to end all wars" under the man who had won it. It was
a perfect opportunity.

Ike threw himself into the job of writing the guidebook with enthusiasm. Maps, pictures, statistical data, and chronological information were heaped upon him, yet he was able to write a cohesive document in four or five months that won the praise of General Pershing.

A month later, in September, 1927, Ike was assigned to the Army War College, the top postgraduate school the army has to offer. At the college, carefully selected officers being groomed for top command positions studied the larger problems of war—supply, movements of troops, relationships with allies, and the grand, overall strategy.

The Eisenhowers lived at the Wyoming Apartments during their stay in Washington and enjoyed a close association with other officers and their wives whom they had known during Ike's military career and with whom he was now studying.

The Eisenhower quarters, wherever they were stationed, seemed to become a mecca for their friends and, many times, a modest apartment or home on a base became Club Eisenhower. Both of them liked having people around and at a party, Mamie was gay and vivacious and played the piano for any group who wanted to sing. Mamie was considered an asset in the secluded society of army officers and their families.

As was expected by his associates and family, Eisenhower did well at the War College. After graduation he accepted another tour of duty with the Battle Monuments Commission, receiving an assignment in Paris, France. Their apartment on the Quai d'Auteuil once again became the social center for visiting friends. Their young son, John, now six, began his formal education at the MacJannet School and life became a pleasant, uncomplicated routine.

Major Eisenhower's duties were not difficult. He studied the terrain between the Moselle and Rhine rivers, driving back and forth over country that was still pockmarked by shell holes and old trenches. He memorized French railroads and highways and the countryside in general. This information was useful to him when he later became Allied commander.

Meanwhile the Eisenhowers traveled throughout Europe on

holidays, becoming familiar with other countries as well as France, and then returned to the United States in November, 1929. Now thirty-nine years old, Major Eisenhower had hoped to get a command of his own. But once again he was a staff officer, assigned as assistant executive in the office of the assistant secretary of war.

His job was "the supervision of the procurement of all military supplies and other business of the War Department . . . for the mobilization of materiel and industrial organizations essential to wartime needs." In layman's language, his job was to smooth the way for cooperation between American industry and the War Department should there be another war.

But most Americans were not worried about a future war at this time. They were more concerned about the crash of the stock market, which had taken place shortly before the Eisenhowers returned. They were concerned about unemployment, about income, even about food. War was not their immediate concern. Survival was.

Ike's job was not particularly interesting, but he persevered, interviewing many leaders of industry and government and then writing a plan for industrial mobilization which was widely read and praised by associates and superior officers.

One of them was General Douglas MacArthur, who immediately assigned Eisenhower to his staff. General MacArthur was an unusual man, self-centered and self-confident to an extreme but thought by many to be a genius.

His army career had been highly successful. He had scored the highest scholastic record ever achieved at West Point, commanded a division in France during World War I, been the superintendent for West Point after the war, and now he was chief of staff.

Eisenhower and MacArthur were totally opposite in temperament and approach to life, and it is doubtful if they actually liked each other. But each respected the other's talents. Eisenhower said of his superior officer ". . . he had a brain." And, as early as 1931, MacArthur predicted that Eisenhower would become a top military leader in the next war.

Lieutenant Colonel and Mrs. Eisenhower with their son John at Rock Creek Park, Washington, D.C., 1934.

Ike made the best of his time under MacArthur. He wrote annual reports, speeches, and articles, working with presidential assistants on problems of strategy and international relations. It was another period of intellectual exploration and growth for him, not unnoticed in civilian circles, too. Offered a job by a newspaper as its military editor, he turned it down.

But it was not always this way serving under MacArthur. Eisenhower later recalled that one of the worst moments of his life occurred in the summer of 1932 when he was ordered to help drive the Bonus Marchers out of Washington.

The marchers were World War I veterans, now unemployed in the Great Depression. They wanted early payment on the bonus promised them for wartime services. Although many leaders of the day, including MacArthur, felt the marchers were a threat to law and order, Eisenhower did not. Furthermore, he felt they should be treated with every consideration.

Nevertheless, in July, President Hoover ordered the police and the army to drive the marchers out of the city. MacArthur personally led the soldiers into the encampment of shacks where the veterans lived and drove them out. Fortunately, no one was injured. Afterwards, MacArthur took much of the blame for the entire messy business, which seemed not to bother him a bit. He seemed to enjoy controversy even as Eisenhower disliked it.

In 1935, MacArthur completed his tour of duty as chief of staff and accepted a position in the Philippines, a colony of the United States whose independence had been guaranteed to begin in 1946, at which time it would need a defense force. Manuel L. Quezon, president of the colony, hired MacArthur to train an army for him.

MacArthur asked Eisenhower to join him, but the major was reluctant, feeling he had been a staff officer long enough. MacArthur prevailed, however, and in September, twenty years after Eisenhower's first request to go there had been denied, he sailed for the Philippines.

MacArthur and Eisenhower's strategies for a new Philippine army were limited in two major areas, arms and money. Eisen-

Christmas Party, 1938. Manila, Philippines. Left to right: Eisenhower, Mrs. MacArthur, Paul McNutt, government official, Mamie Eisenhower, and Douglas MacArthur.

hower drafted so many plans that were rejected by President Quezon that he said at one point, "They also serve who only draft and draft."

While in the Philippines, Eisenhower had another opportunity to leave the military and return to civilian life. But he was reluctant to resign from the army. He felt his destiny was with the armed forces, particularly now that Adolf Hitler was becoming an unsettling force in Europe.

After Hitler attacked Poland in September, 1939, Eisenhower asked to return to the United States. MacArthur tried to persuade him to stay in the Philippines, but Eisenhower insisted. He had missed combat duty during World War I; he would not miss it in the war that he felt would soon involve his country again.

4

Getting Ready

As the Eisenhowers sailed back to the United States, they had quiet moments to reflect on the period in their lives just ending. The Philippine tour had been another time of growth and change. John had gone there just before his fourteenth birthday. Now he was thinking about college. His father, promoted to lieutenant colonel during his stay, had once again proven himself with his show of intellectual strength and military knowledge. Although he and MacArthur differed and disagreed on many issues, Eisenhower had won MacArthur's respect. It was respect that was hard-earned from a man who thought of himself as the world's finest soldier.

Everyone was impressed with Eisenhower, especially President Quezon of the Philippines. He did everything, within limits, to persuade the Eisenhowers to stay on in his country, offering a blank check with the amount to be filled in by the Eisenhowers. The only tangible gift that Eisenhower would accept was the Philippine Distinguished Service Star, given to him during a luncheon ceremony that included Quezon's speech expressing admiration and gratitude. A proud Mamie pinned it on Ike's jacket.

Back in the States, Eisenhower held a variety of jobs in the following year of 1940. The army was expanding rapidly and new recruits needed to be trained and equipped. One of his first assignments was to plan the movement of all troops in the Fourth Army area, which included the entire West Coast and Northwest.

During this assignment, which was to Ford Ord, California, and then to Fort Lewis, Washington, Eisenhower came into contact

Mamie Eisenhower pins Distinguished Service Star of the Philippines on Dwight Eisenhower, December 12, 1939, at Malacanan Palace, Manila. It was presented by President Manuel Quezon.

On maneuvers at Fort Lewis, Washington, 1941, with fellow officers, Eisenhower in center.

with many old friends again. Major Mark Clark was one officer he'd known and liked for years. General John L. DeWitt was another. He knew General George C. Marshall, now chief of staff, slightly, but had heard of him for years by reputation. Paths crossed in the army, then crossed and crossed again. And always, officers knew who their most talented fellow officers were, where they were, and what they were doing. This seemed to be a time when many military eyes were following Eisenhower.

By the end of June, Great Britain's Royal Air Force was battling Nazi Germany's Luftwaffe for control of the skies over London. It seemed as if it was the last stand for Europe. France had recently fallen and so had the rest of the European community.

By early fall, the United States began to prepare for the inevitable. President Franklin Delano Roosevelt, running for an unprecedented third term, took action by trading fifty American destroyers to the British in exchange for American bases on British property. A program of lend-lease was approved by Congress. But the main concentration of the government was focused on preparing military personnel for action in the shortest time possible. The National Guard was called up and a selective service system began.

In October, Ike received a letter from George Patton, his friend from the Tank Corps days. Patton expected to get command of a tank division soon and wanted Ike to be a regimental commander under him. This seemed to be a unique opportunity for someone who had longed for troop command experience. Until his return to the United States, Eisenhower had served directly with troops for only six months in the past eighteen years.

Then a telegram came from the War Department asking him to return to Washington for a staff assignment. Ike agonized over it, and soon his agony became physical. He broke out in a case of shingles, a disease brought on by nerves and anxiety.

Finally he replied to the request, stating that an individual's preference should have little weight in determining his assignment, but that if his own wishes were considered, he would rather go anywhere but Washington. This worked; he stayed at Fort Lewis with the troops and was given even more responsibility.

Fort Lewis was good duty for the Eisenhower family. Ike's brother, Edgar, lived nearby in Tacoma. Now a successful lawyer, he had no children of his own, so he began to take a paternal interest in his nephew, John. One day, Edgar told him that he would finance his college education if John would study law. Then Edgar would take him into his firm and one day turn over the business to him.

If Ike had personal wishes for his son's future, he didn't express them. Instead, he did as his mother had done before him. He let John choose for himself.

In reality, John's choice may already have been made for him by his father, though in action, not in words. John had watched his father devote himself to a military career for many years, turning down numerous civilian positions that could have made him a wealthy man. John must have concluded that his father had a strong reason for remaining in the service of his country. He was respected and well-liked but not well-off financially and certainly not as high in rank as many of his peers. And there had been disappointments—John was old enough to understand that.

Ike later remarked, "My ambition in the army was to make everybody I worked for regretful when I was ordered to other duty."

That must have been apparent to John. Ike liked what he did, found the respect he needed, and enjoyed serving his country. That was enough for John. The following winter he took the entrance exam for West Point, passed with a high score, and made plans to enter the following summer. He had chosen a career in the army.

Lieutenant Colonel Eisenhower was promoted to full colonel now. Before he had time to settle into his newest job at Fort Lewis, he was ordered to Fort Sam Houston to become chief of staff of the Third Army under General Walter Kreuger. On their twenty-fifth wedding anniversary in July, 1941, Ike and Mamie returned to the place where they'd met so long ago.

But he wasn't around very long. Soon he was gone to Louisiana to take part in the biggest peacetime war exercises in the nation's history. More than four hundred thousand officers and men of the Second and Third Armies converged to wage a war that was real in every respect except for weapons and the enemy. Everyone was deadly serious—these war games would show the War Department how well-prepared the army was for the real thing.

Eisenhower had planned, organized, and now was executing the maneuvers for the Third Army. It was said that he was everywhere in the field, changing strategy, improvising, and innovating new opportunities. No detail escaped him, and he hardly slept.

When it was over, the Third Army had won a clear victory over the Second, and newspapers soon heard of Ike's role. For the first time since his football-playing days at West Point, his name and photograph appeared in the news media. A nation-

On maneuvers in Louisiana, fall, 1941.

ally syndicated newspaper column stated, "Colonel Eisenhower . . . conceived and directed the strategy that routed the Second Army."

In September he was promoted to brigadier general and wore his first star. He could hardly believe it. He wrote his friend, General Leonard Gerow: "One thing is certain—when they get clear down to my place on the list, they are passing out stars with considerable abandon."

Ike continued to work hard at Fort Sam Houston that fall, putting in long days. On Sunday, December 7, he went to the office as usual, but came home for a nap in the afternoon, telling Mamie that he didn't want to be disturbed for any reason. His Sunday afternoon nap wasn't the only one to be interrupted that day by the Japanese attack on the United States fleet stationed at Pearl Harbor.

A few days later he received a telephone call from Colonel Walter Bedell Smith, then secretary to the Joint Chiefs of Staff. He said, "The Chief [Marshall] says for you to hop a plane and get up here to Washington right away. Tell your boss that formal orders will come through later."

If Ike was disappointed to be going to another desk job, he had no time to think about it. The weather and the war combined to give his travel plans a few problems, and he got to Washington as best he could, first by plane and then by train.

But it was the last time in his life he had to concern himself with his own travel plans. It was also the last time he went anywhere as a relatively unknown individual. When he stepped off the train in Washington, D.C. early on the morning of Sunday, December 14, he left obscurity behind forever.

5

The War Begins

Washington had been a quiet, southern city during Eisenhower's last tour of duty from 1927 to 1935. Now it was jammed with extra people involved with the brand-new war. Hotel rooms were at a premium, restaurants were always full, and people worked around the clock. There was a frantic effort under way to do something about the outrage committed at Pearl Harbor just a week before.

But when Brigadier General Eisenhower entered the Munitions Building on that December morning, officers were approaching their work in an atmosphere of professional determination and calm. And none more so than Chief of Staff General George C. Marshall. He set the businesslike pace.

Eisenhower wondered what Marshall wanted him to do and the answer wasn't long in coming. Marshall didn't engage in small talk.

In fifteen or twenty minutes, Marshall summarized the conditions. Much of the Pacific fleet had been lost at Pearl Harbor except for the aircraft carriers, and most of the army air force had been destroyed in the Philippines. The Japanese were threatening Hong Kong and Singapore and had already landed on the island of Luzon. With Japanese superiority established on the sea and in the air, the Philippines were virtually cut off from the rest of the world.

Eisenhower was eager to learn more about the conditions in the islands. He and Mamie had left many friends there among army personnel and civilians. Marshall reviewed statistics indicating that only about thirty thousand Philippine and American soldiers were left to defend the islands, and that their supplies were very low.

Now Marshall abruptly asked, "What should be our general line of action?"

Eisenhower realized he was being tested and that his answer could affect his military future. But the question was so all-encompassing that he couldn't respond without reflective thought.

He asked for a few hours and found a desk with a typewriter and some paper. Then he sat down and began to peck out his answer. All of his training and personal feelings were reflected in his reply.

In direct, no-nonsense prose, he outlined the steps to be taken: First, a base should be built up in Australia from which supplies and personnel could be moved to the Philippines. He wrote that fighter planes, bombers, and ammunition could be ferried to Australia, knowing that it would be some time before major reinforcements could get to the fighting men. It might already be too late to save the Philippines. Then he made his most important point. "The people of China, the Philippines, and the Dutch East Indies will be watching us. They may excuse failure, but they will not excuse abandonment. . . . We must take great risks and spend any amount of money required."

What Eisenhower didn't know, as he typed away, was that Marshall had already decided, with President Roosevelt's concurrence, that this was exactly what should be done. A little while later Marshall gave Eisenhower command of the Philippines and Far Eastern Section of the War Plans Division.

A strong partnership began to build immediately between Marshall and Eisenhower. From December, 1941, until the war ended in August, 1945, they would work closely together, one setting the broad policies and making strategic decisions, the other translating those policies and decisions into action.

The United States was now at war on a global scale. Three days after Pearl Harbor, Germany and Italy declared war on the U.S. Of the three Axis powers, Japan, Italy, and Germany, the last was by far the strongest. It had been preparing for war since the midthirties and its well-trained and well-equipped army was led by professionals. In two years it had overrun much of Europe and then turned east, opening a second front earlier in 1941 by declaring war on Russia. Under Adolf Hitler's fanatic leadership, the Germans seemed unbeatable. In the first three months of the war with Russia, they captured over two million prisoners.

In late December, British Prime Minister Winston Churchill came to meet President Roosevelt for the first time and also to take part in a joint conference on war strategy. Marshall was also a participant and he brought Eisenhower along to meet the British contingent.

At this conference the basic strategy of the war was soon established and, in a paper he prepared for Marshall to present, Eisenhower wrote: "The strength of the Allied defenses in the entire theater would be greatly increased through single, intelligent command."

Churchill later told his chiefs of staff that he was not convinced this plan was workable or desirable, but that he had to meet the American view. "We are no longer single but married," he told Clement Atlee, a member of his cabinet.

Finally it was agreed that a committee called the Combined Chiefs of Staff would supervise Anglo-American activities during the war. The way was now clear for a single officer to lead the combined forces in Europe. Eisenhower had been instrumental in writing the description for the most important job of his military career.

Mamie arrived in Washington in February, 1942, and she and Ike moved into a suite at the Wardman Park Hotel until their house at Fort Myer would be ready. Before she came, Ike had stayed with his brother, Milton, and his wife at their suburban home. He worked such long hours that he later remarked he never saw their home in daylight. Now with Mamie there he tried to keep his working day down to twelve or fifteen hours.

Even before Eisenhower became chief of the War Plans Division, succeeding his old friend, General Gerow, he realized that the United States had to focus its energy on only one front. Al-

Brigadier General Eisenhower with Brigadier General Robin Crawford and Brigadier General Leonard Gerow at War Plans Division, War Department, Washington, D.C., January 23, 1942.

though feelings ran high against the Japanese and there was a general cry to counterattack in the Pacific, Europe had to be the first focus of most major military activity.

There were two reasons. Russia and Japan were not at war and England had few supply centers in the Far East, so the United States would have to go it alone in the Pacific. With defeat imminent in the Philippines and most of the Pacific already in Japanese hands, any effort there might prove to be too much right now. The Pacific theater had not been abandoned, just postponed.

In Europe, however, the Russians were battling the Germans on one front while the British were battling them on another. In addition, England could also provide land bases from which to launch a massive invasion of the continent.

One disturbing thought arose in military and civilian leaders' minds at this time. Many people felt that a German victory over the Russians might be acceptable. Senator Harry Truman remarked that the best outcome would be for Germany and Russia to beat each other to death. Others were saying that Americans should not waste any effort or resources to help Russia.

Eisenhower tried to stop this kind of talk. Although he was anti-Communist, he knew that the real enemy in Europe now was Germany and it was against this nation that all effort should be directed. He also knew that it would take much longer to defeat the Germans without the help of the Red Army.

Eisenhower wanted to make plans for an invasion of Europe that could take place as early as the fall of 1942. He felt it would help Russia's situation and keep that country in the war. The leaders of Britain were not so sure that the Allies were ready for such a monumental task, however, and counterproposed with the idea that North Africa or Norway be invaded instead.

On March 10, David Eisenhower died in Kansas, but the general was so busy that he could not go to his father's funeral. He mourned his loss by writing on his calendar pad the following day, "I have felt terribly. I should like so much to be with my Mother these few days. But we're at war! And war is not soft—it has no time to indulge even the deepest and most sacred emotions. I loved my Dad."

Perhaps because his father's death had made him more aware of his own family, Eisenhower took a weekend away from his duties at the end of March. He and Mamie spent his first days off in months visiting their son, John, at West Point.

He returned to find he'd been recommended for promotion to major general. He now had his second star and soon would be named assistant chief of staff in charge of the Operations Division.

The Combined Chiefs of Staff spent much of the early part of 1942 arguing about whether to attack Europe or North Africa that fall. Finally, in June, they were able to agree on a number of things. Plan One would be an attempt at landing on the coast of France if Russia appeared to be on the point of surrendering. If the Russians did not capitulate, the Allies would launch their main invasion in the spring of 1943. By then American industry should have turned out enough equipment and munitions to supply this effort.

In April General Marshall went to London to discuss these plans in more detail. When he returned to Washington, he ordered Eisenhower to England for further talks with the Allies.

The second front idea was still being coolly received by the British, although they warmed to Eisenhower's personality immediately. During one conference, Ike said his choice for commander in charge of combined operations was Admiral Louis Mountbatten, British chief of Joint Operations. He said that he found Mountbatten was "vigorous, intelligent, and courageous."

An uneasy silence followed before a British general said, "Possibly you have not met Admiral Mountbatten. There he is, sitting directly across the table from you."

Eisenhower took the laughter which followed in a goodnatured manner, thus impressing the British even more. This meeting between Mountbatten and Eisenhower was the beginning of a lifelong friendship.

Marshall now asked Eisenhower to write the directive for the American commander in these proposed operations and to create the U.S. Army's European theater of operations (ETO). Eisenhower completed the thirty-page draft early in June and said to Marshall that it was one paper he should read carefully before it went out because it was likely to be important in the war effort.

Marshall replied, "I certainly do want to read it. You may be the man who executes it. If that's the case, when can you leave?" Eisenhower replied, "Tomorrow."

Three days later, Marshall called him into his office and said, "You're going to command American forces in the European theater." Eisenhower was too stunned to reply.

On his calendar pad dated June 11, Eisenhower wrote, "The C/S says I'm the guy. . . . Now we really go to work."

There was much to be done officially before he left. Still Eisenhower managed to find time to spend with Mamie and John, who had come down from West Point on a military pass during his father's final weekend. Eisenhower also called his mother in Abilene for a farewell conversation.

When he met with Marshall to be dismissed from his duties in Washington, his friend and commander gave him some final words of advice: "Persuade by accomplishment rather than by eloquence."

Eisenhower went to Bolling Field early on a Tuesday morning in June, 1942. His family was not there to see him leave; it just wasn't his way. Later, when the plane took off and circled over Fort Myer, Eisenhower looked down to see a slight, feminine figure standing by the flagpole. He smiled and watched until he could no longer see Mamie on the parade ground below. It would be 1944 before he saw her again.

6

Taking Command

The day after Eisenhower arrived in London, he held a press conference to announce that he had assumed leadership of the American armed forces in Europe. He had stepped directly into the spotlight on a world stage, and people were eager to know about him. Where had he come from? What had he done before? What was his family like? What plans did he have to end the war?

Curiosity was not the only motivation of reporters who gathered around General Ike. They were immediately impressed by his down-to-earth, friendly manner and genuinely liked him. He was at once completely open and direct; he was not playing the public relations game.

He was so good at communicating with the press that his public relations officer later remarked Eisenhower really didn't need him. How the general did it was no secret. He was simply himself.

Eisenhower dressed as the soldier he was: trim, tailored, neat. No grandiose, specially-made uniforms like MacArthur. He acted in an uncomplicated manner, too. He was sincere, patriotic, and modest.

And there was that face. He was not only photogenic but very expressive. Whether displaying anger, surprise, or happiness, he gave photographers an excellent opportunity for a photo that had a good chance of winning a front-page, two-column spread in their hometown papers.

His family would soon be caught up in the glare of publicity as well. Mamie was asked for countless interviews and she received thousands of letters, which she answered herself. Many requests came for her appearance at patriotic rallies. She tried to avoid most social gatherings, however. During the course of the war, she would give anonymous free time to soldiers' canteens.

John found that his classmates at West Point began to treat him differently. After all, his dad was the general in charge over there. John enjoyed the attention but also asked that he be treated as one of the cadets, the way he had been before his father had assumed leadership.

Reporters and photographers now descended on Abilene, wanting to know all about General Ike's life there. They soon found that Ida Eisenhower was good copy. When his mother was asked the question, "How does it feel to have a famous son?" her quick answer was, "Which one?"

General Eisenhower began to use the press and their attention to sell the idea of unity among the Allies. He knew it was important to rally the tired British and to inform the Americans at home of what was happening overseas. Above all, he wanted to promote a spirit of friendship and good will among the nations coming together to fight Germany.

His immediate problem, however, was to put together an official family. Lieutenant Commander Harry Butcher, an old friend he'd met through his brother, Milton, became his unofficial public relations officer and personal aide. Mickey McKeough, the orderly assigned to him at Fort Sam Houston after he became a colonel, had come with him to England. Lieutenant Ernest R. Lee was his executive officer, and soon General Walter Bedell Smith became his chief of staff.

When the general arrived in London, a suite of rooms was waiting for him at Claridge's, but he found it too fancy for his tastes. He moved to another hotel, but felt it was too public. He wanted a place where he could escape his fishbowl existence, and Butcher soon rented Telegraph Cottage in Surrey for him. There the general could escape on occasional weekends without being seen or followed, sometimes playing golf, and reading his favorite Wild West novels in the evening.

Most of the time he worked. He stated that he wanted to form "the best army that the United States has ever put into the field" and he believed that discipline, training, and morale were essential to his task.

It was some task, however, and he drove himself to it. American soldiers were coming into England in ever-increasing numbers, and he spent much more of his time visiting them. He urged them out into the fields for training, stressing the importance of preparedness and knowledge of equipment.

He also worked hard to build teamwork and fellowship between the American enlisted man and his British counterpart. GIs (the nickname for American soldiers) came to England as the highest-paid and best-fed soldiers in the world. They were inclined to spend money freely in public and also complain about living conditions and food. This gave the British, who had already sacrificed much, a feeling the American soldiers were immature and spoiled. A popular English saying at the time was, "The trouble with the Yanks is that they are overpaid, oversexed, overfed, and over here."

Eisenhower set out to change the image of the GIs. He suggested they spend part of their pay on War Bonds, instructed them on how much the British had sacrificed for the war effort, and saw to it that they became better acquainted with their host country. He then made each commander responsible for the men under him by saying, ". . . we are here not as muddling amateurs but as earnest, competent soldiers who know what we are about." Soon the British would agree.

Meanwhile, the summer of 1942 was going badly for the Allies on all war fronts. MacArthur had been ordered to leave the Philippines in March and escaped to Australia. Left behind, though, were American and Philippine soldiers who were soon killed or captured on Bataan and Corregidor. Now all of the Pacific theater was under Japanese control.

On the other side of the world, German submarines patrolling the Atlantic were sinking American shipping at an alarming rate. Further, it looked as if the Russians couldn't hold on much longer and the Russian dictator, Joseph Stalin, was threatening to make peace with Germany if a second front was not opened soon.

Eisenhower continued to push for a cross-channel surprise attack either in 1942 or early in 1943. But the British still refused to go along with a plan to invade France, saying it was too suicidal. Indeed, the chances of success were thought to be only 20 percent and the British, led by Prime Minister Winston Churchill, favored attacking on another front and gradually encircling the Germans on the continent. Churchill called it "closing the ring."

Eisenhower and Marshall were reluctant to go along with a lesser target such as Norway or Africa. They felt the armies would be so tied down that the main invasion plan would then be impossible by 1943. It would probably mean postponing the invasion until 1944.

Through most of July, Eisenhower and Churchill argued their countries' positions. Toward the end of the month, Marshall and other members of the Joint Chiefs of Staff came to England for a meeting with their British counterparts. They were deadlocked until Churchill conferred with Roosevelt, and the American president ordered Marshall to put troops into action in 1942. On July 22, Marshall told the Combined Chiefs of Staff he would go along with the invasion of Africa, since he considered Norway too risky.

Eisenhower was upset, saying later that "July 22 could well go down as the blackest day in history." After all his work on both invasion plans, they were thrown out and he had to start again on a new operation. Good soldier that he was, however, he proceeded, working harder than ever to make the new plan succeed.

The new operation was code-named TORCH, and the Combined Chiefs of Staff made Eisenhower its commander. He was promoted to lieutenant general and now wore his third star.

The plan called for British-American forces to land in French-controlled Algeria and Morocco, then move east to Tunisia where they would join with the British Eighth Army, under General Bernard Montgomery, who would be coming west from Egypt.

Complications began to arise almost immediately. There had not been a sea-to-shore invasion in recent military history, so there were no successes—or failures—for Eisenhower to study. He could only count on his own knowledge and expertise and hope for the best.

Other complications arose. Eisenhower would be commanding navies and air forces as well as armies—another first. They would be not only American but British, another unprecedented step. One thing he felt certain of, if the two nations did not get along well during this invasion, all would be lost including, most likely, the war.

More problems included training and logistics. The soldiers arriving in England were raw recruits. Time was short to train these men for a major invasion and battle. Transporting them and their supplies to Africa required more than a thousand ships. And landing them two thousand miles away on little-known terrain was a further complication.

One of the major headaches of the campaign was the French political problem. No one was sure if the French in Algeria would be hostile or helpful during the invasion. Since France had been overthrown by Germany in 1940, a pro-Nazi government at Vichy controlled unoccupied France and its possessions in Africa.

Eisenhower needed a French leader who could be counted on to defy Vichy and cooperate with the Allies in Africa. Churchill and Roosevelt became involved in the selection of that leader as communications were radioed back and forth from London to Washington. One candidate was General Charles de Gaulle, leader of the Free French government in London. Roosevelt vetoed him because of a personal dislike. Also it was thought that government officials in Algeria would not welcome de Gaulle's leadership because he had called them traitors.

Thoughts now turned to two other Frenchmen, General Henri Giraud and Admiral Jean-François Darlan. Churchill and Roosevelt agreed with Eisenhower that either man could be "our chief collaborator." Finally, Giraud was chosen and was asked to rally the French soldiers in Algeria to the Allied cause. He indicated he would comply.

Eisenhower wrote to his friend General Patton, "I feel like the lady in the circus that has to ride three horses with no very good idea of exactly where any one of the three is going to go."

❦ On November 4, 1942, General Eisenhower flew to Gibraltar to set up command post headquarters. The invasion began four days later when more than one hundred thousand men and fourteen squadrons of fighter planes moved on Casablanca in Morocco on the Atlantic coast, and on Oran and Algiers in Algeria on the Mediterranean Sea.

General Giraud flew to Algiers and ordered the French forces to cease fire. The French soldiers paid no attention to him; Giraud was not their legitimate superior. The French continued to resist the Allied invasion.

After several days of fighting between the French and the Allies, Eisenhower appealed to Admiral Jean-Francois Darlan, commander-in-chief of Vichy's armed forces, to order a cease-fire. Darlan cooperated and the French soldiers stopped fighting because they considered Darlan their legitimate superior. Eisenhower believed that now the Allies could get down to the business of fighting the Germans.

But the French problem wasn't over. In England and the United States, Eisenhower was roundly criticized because Darlan was considered a fascist. He represented everything the Allies were fighting against. General de Gaulle was furious that he had not been consulted, and asked if the Allies were going to make deals with all the fascist leaders.

Eisenhower continued to be criticized as he explained his position. If he had not brought in Darlan, the French would have continued to fight the Allies. Now if he turned his back on Darlan, the French would fight the Allies again. He had ignored the political implications, concentrating instead on military needs. He was, after all, a military man, not a politician.

Rumors flew that Eisenhower was going to be fired over the Darlan matter, possibly ending his career. He knew, however, that Churchill and Roosevelt would also be held accountable since they had approved making either Darlan or Giraud "our chief collaborator." Finally cooler heads took charge, knowing that the Allies couldn't afford to lose a commander of Eisenhower's caliber, and he went on with the war.

General Eisenhower soon discovered that the time spent in dealing with Darlan and subsequent political storms had cost the Allied drive in Africa precious time. A golden opportunity to rid Algeria and Tunisia of the German army had been lost. Not until mid-November could Eisenhower send an army toward Tunisia to join forces with the British Eighth Army under General Bernard Montgomery and attempt to squeeze the German Afrika Korps under Field Marshal Erwin Rommel between them. Rommel was one of Germany's most skilled generals, nicknamed the Desert Fox by his enemies.

The weather, increased German resistance and supply problems slowed the Allied troops as they cautiously moved toward Tunisia. By now, Eisenhower had moved his base of operations from Gibraltar to Algiers to be closer to the fighting. He could go to the advancing front lines and see firsthand what needed to be done.

On December 22, Eisenhower went to the front to see how soon a new attack could be mounted. It was the same old story. Steady rain had turned the countryside into fields of gluelike mud. He decided to call off an attack to wait for better weather and reinforcements.

Eisenhower was sitting down to dinner on Christmas Eve with staff officers of the British First Army when he was told that Darlan had been assassinated. Worried that the French soldiers fighting along with the Allies might now desert, Eisenhower began immediately the thirty-hour return trip to Algiers.

When he arrived, he learned that a young Frenchman had shot the general. Whether a conspiracy to install a new French coalition or simply vengeance by an individual, the mystery of Darlan's death was never solved. The assassin was executed without being questioned. General Giraud replaced Darlan and the French troops remained loyal to the Allies.

In mid-January, 1943, President Roosevelt and Prime Minister Churchill came to Casablanca for a conference that would last ten days. Eisenhower attended to report on the situation in Africa and was promoted to a four-star general at the same time.

He then was told to give the Tunisian campaign the full attention of the Allied forces. Asked when he thought victory would be a possibility, Eisenhower impulsively replied, "May 15."

He had two major problems to solve first. The primitive roads of Africa continued to be impassable much of the time. Rain turned them into a quagmire, and supplies were often short because they could not be transported to the front lines.

Lack of experience by soldiers and officers was the other pressing problem. Often the Allies were outflanked, outthought, and outfought by the Germans.

Meanwhile the Germans were taking full advantage of the situation and threatening everywhere. Rommel decided to attack at the Allies' most vulnerable point, the Kasserine Pass. If the Germans could break through here, he felt they could drive on to Algiers and force the Allies into the sea.

Eisenhower visited his troops daily, offering suggestions to the commanders in charge, complaining about the positions of the soldiers, and urging everyone to be alert. Yet he issued no direct orders. He expected the officers in charge to issue them.

In February, Rommel's troops attacked the Kasserine Pass, opening a wide gap in Allied lines. For two days German troops rushed forward as Allied soldiers ran from the attack, waiting for reinforcements that never came. The Ninth Division started on a 735-mile march for the front but arrived too late to do much good.

By the third day, however, it became obvious that Rommel was running out of supplies. He would soon, in fact, retreat to his earlier lines.

The Kasserine Pass was a costly but valuable lesson for Eisenhower and his troops. First, the soldiers learned how very real and very tough the enemy was. They also learned they didn't like to be kicked around by the enemy. Eisenhower learned more than anyone else. He found out that no fighting unit, even those on the front lines, should ever stop training. Constant readiness was necessary to success. From then on, training became a continuing part of the soldier's life under Ike. He also learned to get tough with his commanding officers. He fired the officer in charge of the

General Eisenhower with General George S. Patton, Jr. at his headquarters in Tunisia, March 16, 1943.

Second Army which had been routed at the Kasserine Pass and replaced him with his old friend, General George S. Patton, Jr.

Patton was a spirited man and a fighter. He shook up the Second Army, beginning a series of tough training programs before he launched small-scale attacks on the Germans.

In the following months, the British Eighth Army under General Montgomery, and the Second Army led by Patton, drove the Germans back to their last strongholds near Tunis. When it appeared that victory by the Allies would be forthcoming, Patton was sent back to Algiers to assist in plans for the invasion of Sicily. Another old friend of Eisenhower's, General Omar Bradley, replaced Patton and began the final assault on the German army.

The British feared that the Americans lacked the necessary experience to deliver the knockout blow. Eisenhower insisted that the American troops be placed in a position where they could test themselves. He reasoned that if they were not confident of their ability now, how could they stand up to the job still to come in Europe?

Bradley and the Second Army were given the hardest job and, on April 30, they attacked the Germans at a strategic place called Hill 609. If Bradley's troops could break through here, the German army would have no place to go but into the sea.

After a fierce fight, with Bradley's Second Army attacking from one direction and the British coming from another, the defeat of the Germans was assured. On May 7, Bradley sent the message, "Mission accomplished." Eisenhower had accomplished his mission, too, by defeating the German army in Africa before his targeted date of May 15.

A week later a total of 275,000 German prisoners had been captured. American troops discovered they could fight and General Eisenhower discovered he could command. Messages poured in from friends, leaders, and private citizens, offering congratulations. As nice as it was to be appreciated for this victory, he didn't dwell on it long. Even as he reviewed the victorious troops in Tunis, his mind was elsewhere. General Eisenhower already had begun to plan the summer invasion of Sicily.

7

The Next Move

The Combined Chiefs of Staff met in Washington in May, 1943, to decide the Allies' next move. For two weeks they argued and finally agreed to a cross-channel invasion in 1944. Meanwhile they reached no decision on where to go in the Mediterranean after the invasion of Sicily. No one was satisfied with this non-decision, however. Shortly after the Washington meeting, Churchill and a delegation, including Marshall, flew to Algeria to meet with Eisenhower. Churchill argued for the invasion of Italy after Sicily. Others argued different tactics. Eisenhower pondered all their suggestions but kept his own counsel. He was given the final authority to decide what to do after Sicily.

French political problems bothered him even as he planned the invasion. General de Gaulle was a proud, sensitive man who demanded responsibility and attention. President Roosevelt was not convinced of his importance to the Allies. It became Eisenhower's job to convince him otherwise. After a series of agonizing arguments with the president, Eisenhower persuaded him to allow de Gaulle to take command of the French government in North Africa. Eisenhower seemed to be the one friend de Gaulle had among Allied leaders.

Plans for the invasion, which was scheduled to begin on July 10, 1943, were now well under way. More than a thousand offices were occupied in Algiers by military men planning this invasion, which would become the largest amphibious attack thus far in history.

There was much to do in a short time. Mountains of supplies

General Marshall meets with Eisenhower at Allied Headquarters in Algeria, June 3, 1943.

had to be gathered and a fleet of three thousand ships assembled. Men in Patton's Seventh Army and Montgomery's Eighth needed to be trained to lead the invasion. More arguments followed, this time between Patton and Montgomery over the best invasion maneuvers. Finally Montgomery won out with his plan for the armies to go ashore side by side on the southeastern coast of the island.

A project this large did not go undetected by the press, so Eisenhower decided to try something different. Rather than allow newsmen to speculate on the target of the invasion and guess correctly in print, he gathered them together and told them exactly what was going to happen. His associates were shocked, but Ei-

senhower depended on the responsibility of the individual reporters to keep his secret. And it worked. He later said, "No
representative of the press attempted to send out anything that
could possibly be of any value to the enemy."

On July 9, Eisenhower flew to the British-held island of Malta,
midway between Sicily and Africa, to set up command headquarters. His aide, Harry Butcher, noted in his diary that he was
"like a football coach who is pleased that his team is keyed up for
a big game."

On the day before the invasion the weather turned bad. Heavy
winds piled up landing craft, and members of Eisenhower's staff
suggested that the invasion be postponed. Marshall sent a wire
asking if the invasion was on or off and Eisenhower wired back,
"I wish I knew."

After studying new meteorological information, Ike decided to
proceed. Then he watched as the transport planes flew off to Sicily.
As he later wrote Mamie, "There is no use denying that I feel
the strain."

The troops landed without incident. Italian soldiers surrendered
easily, but the German soldiers began to fight with their usual
skill. As a result, Montgomery's advance was slowed to a crawl
as he and Patton argued about the best way to proceed. Finally
Patton struck out on his own toward Palermo, then advanced on
Messina, which had been the original goal of both the British
Eighth and the American Seventh Armies. Montgomery's actions
were roundly criticized by staff officers. They said that if he had
been less hesitant and his forces more mobile, he could have taken
Messina during the first week of the invasion.

On August 17, Patton's army beat Montgomery's to Messina,
but it was not much of a victory. The Germans had escaped across
the Strait of Messina into Italy after holding a half-million Allied
troops in combat for thirty-eight days and inflicting twenty thousand casualties.

Eisenhower knew where he wanted to go next and knew which
generals he wanted in command. First he had to deal with a very
personal problem.

Generals Patton and Eisenhower conferring at Palermo, Sicily, July 31, 1943. Courtesy U.S. Army photo

On the day that Patton's troops reached Messina, Eisenhower was told of a serious incident involving Patton and an enlisted man. A week earlier, Patton had visited a hospital and slapped and berated a young GI he thought was malingering.

Eisenhower read the report and, realizing that Patton could be court-martialed for the offense, ordered a full investigation. He tried to keep the story out of the newspapers because he knew that Patton could be called home for a full inquiry. Eisenhower didn't want that—he needed Patton to help win the war. The story was finally printed and Patton was severely criticized by the public and by Congress.

Eisenhower wrote a long, personal letter to Patton, ordering him to apologize to everyone involved. Having known this proud, unpredictable man for so many years, Eisenhower knew the apology would be cruel punishment. And it was. Later, when Eisenhower wrote his report of the incident to Marshall, he said he hoped that Patton was cured of this kind of behavior.

Eisenhower had no time to relax even though Sicily was now secure. In July he had ordered the bombing of Rome. This was such a shock to the Italian legislature that it overthrew Dictator Benito Mussolini and set up a new government under Pietro Badoglio.

Badoglio contacted the Allies secretly, hoping to take Italy out of the war. He did not want to offend the Germans, however, since eighteen fully equipped German divisions remained in Italy.

Eisenhower saw Badoglio's tentative offer as an opportunity to gain control of Italy without losing soldiers in a bitter offensive such as the one the Allies had just been through. His superiors felt differently, remembering the far-reaching political effects of the Darlan deal. Roosevelt said there would be no more deals with fascists, the Italians must surrender unconditionally.

Badoglio and his government would have none of this as messages flew from Washington and London to Eisenhower, and from Eisenhower to the Italian government. As the wrangling continued, Eisenhower became more upset, knowing that the Germans were building up men and supplies in Italy, preparing to take over if Italy surrendered.

The invasion of Italy was scheduled for September 9, 1943. Shortly before this, Eisenhower and Badoglio worked out a surrender policy which they felt would satisfy everyone. In it, the Allies promised to land paratroopers at the Rome airport to protect the Badoglio government when the invasion began. Now, suddenly, Badoglio didn't want the Allied soldiers; furthermore, he didn't want to announce that the Italians had switched to the side of the Allies.

Eisenhower was incensed when he heard of Badoglio's double cross. He radioed the Italian leader: "I intend to broadcast the existence of the armistice at the hour originally planned. If you . . . fail to cooperate as previously agreed I will publish to the world the full record of this affair."

Ike then made his announcement by radio, and Badoglio also broadcast his, ordering all military action by Italians against the Allies to cease.

The entire episode was over nothing because the Italian army simply wasn't interested in fighting anyone. The soldiers dispersed immediately, shedding their uniforms and disappearing into civilian life. Then the German army rushed into Rome and took over the government without a whisper of resistance from the Italians. Soon the Germans had twenty divisions stationed south of Rome, waiting to see what the Allies would do next.

They didn't have long to wait. On September 9, four divisions of the American Fifth Army under General Mark Clark landed at Salerno. Clark thought there would be little or no resistance, but he didn't know that Field Marshal Rommel and fourteen German divisions were stationed in the hills around the bay. Now, as the Americans came ashore, the Germans pinned them down with a murderous volley. Soon German planes and tanks joined in.

Eisenhower called his staff together quickly, ordering them to send in planes and ships, supplies and reserves to help the men pinned down at Salerno. The situation became desperate; the four divisions would be destroyed if they weren't helped. More soldiers came ashore, planes bombed German positions, and Montgomery's Eighth moved slowly up the peninsula until it made contact with the Fifth a few days later. By nightfall of September 14, disaster had been averted as the Germans began a gradual withdrawal of troops at Salerno. Clark's army moved on Naples and captured it on October 1.

Eisenhower decided to move his headquarters closer to the scene of action, and soon he had settled near Naples. Officers were selecting villas for themselves, and a hunting lodge had been picked out for Eisenhower. It proved to be a poor choice because it was rat- and lice-infested and much too large for the general's taste. He didn't have the conqueror's mentality as did many of his staff officers. In a drive around the Isle of Capri, Eisenhower saw many palatial villas and inquired to whom they belonged. He was told that one of them was his, another belonged to another general, and another was reserved for someone else.

That was too much for Eisenhower, the soldier's general. He designated the area as a rest haven for combat soldiers, not a playground for the brass, and ordered the generals out of their villas at once.

The story circulated quickly among the GIs and they loved him all the more for it. His references to Churchill and Roosevelt as "the big shots" had long delighted enlisted men. They also enjoyed his visits along the front lines because he listened to their grievances and did something about them. Ike enjoyed spectacular popularity with the GIs. And the feeling was mutual. "Our soldiers are wonderful," he wrote to Mamie.

Meanwhile, the move toward Rome was slow. Another beachhead crisis would occur at Anzio, followed by bitter fighting at the village of Cassino. Weather and terrain combined to make airpower, manpower, artillery, and landing craft practically worthless. The Germans, however, used their two-to-one manpower advantage, making each bit of progress by the Allies costly and bloody. It looked as if weather and time were on the side of the Germans. The Allies could do nothing but wait.

Eisenhower was impatient with his life right now. The war was progressing at a snail's pace and he knew he might not be able to finish what he'd started. The rumor was that he was going back to Washington to replace George Marshall as chief of staff. Actually, it was more than a rumor. When Churchill and Roosevelt met at Quebec in August, they agreed that when the cross-channel invasion took place, Marshall would be in charge. As much as Eisenhower wanted to be reunited with Mamie, the thought of sitting out the rest of the war behind a desk filled him with dismay.

At this time, Ike's name was suggested as a possible candidate for president. Republicans were looking for someone to oppose Roosevelt. MacArthur was available and willing. Now Eisenhower's name began to be tossed around, and the noted commentator,

Walter Winchell, broadcast the suggestion that a team of Roosevelt and Eisenhower would be a winning Democratic combination.

Eisenhower's public reply was, "I can scarcely imagine anyone in the United States less qualified than I for any type of political work."

A meeting of the Combined Chiefs of Staff was scheduled for Cairo in late November, 1943. Before the meetings began, Roosevelt met Eisenhower on November 20 and they flew to Tunis to inspect the recent battlefield sites. Their conversation touched on many topics, including the identity of the commander of OVERLORD, the code name given to the cross-channel invasion. Roosevelt explained his position about Marshall, considering it only fair that Marshall finally be given an opportunity to lead a field army. Hearing this, Eisenhower thought his future appointment to Washington had become all but official.

During the conference, Eisenhower flew to Cairo to give a brief presentation on the Mediterranean theater. He explained the problems, complications, and solutions, and his presentation made a good impression on everyone.

Churchill and Roosevelt flew on to Teheran in Iran to confer for the first time with Joseph Stalin. Stalin pressed for an early invasion date and demanded to know who the commander would be. Roosevelt replied that he would make a decision in a few days. Finally, on the last day of the conference, Roosevelt asked General Marshall to write the following message: "From the President to Marshal Stalin. The immediate appointment of General Eisenhower to command of OVERLORD operation has been decided upon."

Roosevelt's decision was based on two factors: he simply could not be without George Marshall by his side in Washington; and Eisenhower had proved himself so successful at molding a team of different nationalities together to win a war that he was the logical choice for the most wanted commander's job in history.

On his way back to Washington, Roosevelt stopped in Tunis to meet briefly with Eisenhower. As they drove off in the general's

Late November, 1943, President Roosevelt and General Eisenhower inspect recent battle sites near Tunis. Courtesy U.S. Army

car, Roosevelt said, "Well, Ike, you are going to command OVER-LORD."

The next day General Marshall retrieved the handwritten note he'd prepared for President Roosevelt. At the bottom he wrote, "Dear Eisenhower, I thought you might like to have this as a memento," and sent it to Ike, who framed the note and kept it in a prominent position on his office wall for the rest of his life.

Now Eisenhower and his staff threw themselves into the monumental task of OVERLORD command. They were eager to go to London but had to remain in the Mediterranean until a new command took over. But everyone was irritable and worn-out, Eisenhower perhaps most of all. Finally he was ordered home by Marshall for a brief vacation.

Although the new supreme commander of OVERLORD had come back to the States for a rest, he wasn't given much time for one. There were endless conferences with military leaders and the president plus dinners and meetings with members of Congress. Eisenhower had left the States eighteen months ago as a little-known military man. He returned a four-star celebrity. Now everyone wanted to meet him.

Mamie and Ike managed a brief private time together and went to West Point for a quick reunion with John. There was also time for a trip to Kansas so Ike could see his mother. He had been warned that her memory had dimmed so he should not expect much from her. Ida surprised them, however, when Ike hugged her. "Why, it's Dwight," she cried.

His two-week furlough ended too soon, with far too little accomplished. Eisenhower was dissatisfied at the way some of his meetings with the other military leaders and the president had gone. Nothing had really been decided. On a personal note, he had just begun to get reacquainted with Mamie when it was time to leave.

But he was eager to begin this new operation, one he'd fought for since the beginning of the war. Now, with a battle-tested team of officers around him, and with his own hard-won field experience, the Eisenhower who returned to London to take up command of OVERLORD was a more confident, serious, and decisive man than the one who had gone there eighteen months before.

8

OVERLORD At Last

When Eisenhower arrived in London, he set up the first head-quarters of SHAEF (Supreme Headquarters, Allied Expedition-ary Force) at 20 Grosvernor Square. He was back in familiar territory. But that was the only similarity to the situation of a year and a half ago. Many differences now existed. First, Ike did not have to prove to the British what he could do. Leaders, both military and political, admired him. In February a group of British officers held a party in his honor and presented him with a silver serving tray as a token of their esteem. In making the presentation, Sir Andrew Cunningham said, ". . . No one will dispute it when I say that no one man has done more to advance the Allied cause." Eisenhower was so moved by this gesture that he could barely respond.

Another difference between 1942 and 1944 was that all the facts of the invasion were known, not open to debate. Simply put, the place was Normandy, the time was May 1, sometime after sunrise.

Most of the plans for OVERLORD had been written before Ike had organized SHAEF. In January, 1943, at the Casablanca Conference, the Combined Chiefs of Staff gave the planning job to British Lieutenant General Frederick E. Morgan. Using Ei-senhower's old invasion plans as a model, Morgan and a British-American staff soon presented a well-thought-out design for the coming invasion.

Immediately Ike began to expand the Morgan plan, enlarging the size of the landing party from three to five divisions. Since he

January, 1944. OVERLORD commanders meet in London, England. Left to right: Omar Bradley, Bertram Ramsey, Arthur Tedder, General Eisenhower, Bernard Montgomery, Traffor Leigh-Mallory, Walter Bedell Smith. Courtesy, U.S. Army

did not have enough landing craft and airplanes yet assigned to carry out this larger invasion, he postponed the targeted date until early June.

Eisenhower continued to be interrupted by the press, visiting VIPs, and unscheduled meetings. He had become such a hero to the Londoners that he could not move about freely. As much as he enjoyed attention from its citizens, London was not a place where he could work.

In February, Eisenhower set up SHAEF headquarters in Bushy Park, a quieter, remote section of the city. And he moved back into Telegraph Cottage, the small home he'd enjoyed during his last stay in England. Occasionally he could even play a few rounds of golf there.

Ike's immediate problem was to convince the officers and leaders around him that all of the Allied air forces should now come under SHAEF control. Few agreed, particularly the British and American air force leaders. They were bombing targets deep within Germany itself and felt this alone would bring Hitler to his knees.

But Eisenhower favored another place to attack the German war machine. If the air forces were brought under his control in OVER-LORD, he could direct the bombing of the French railway system in a manner designed to destroy it. This was called the Transportation Plan.

He met with much resistance in the beginning, but he persisted. Finally the Transportation Plan was approved and carried out during the months before D day, the name given to the invasion date. Even the French people agreed with the plan while knowing that much property and some lives would be lost.

As a result, the railway system of France was on the point of total collapse by late spring, and this proved to be a turning point in the battle for Normandy when the invasion began. The plan succeeded because it isolated the Germans in Normandy. Supplies simply couldn't get to them.

Now, in April, Eisenhower also had to isolate the activity in southern England. If OVERLORD was to be successful, it had to catch the Germans by surprise. A plan was devised to make German spies in England think the Allies would attack Norway and then invade at Pas de Calais, directly across the channel. The Germans were also led to believe that the invasion force would be much larger than it actually was.

Security was the key. Eisenhower insisted that a ban be imposed on diplomatic correspondence leaving England. Decoy troops and materièls were placed along the English and Scottish coasts for the Germans to spy on. Ike also persuaded Churchill to close off the southern coastal area to civilians because of the buildup of real materièls and the training of real soldiers occurring there.

Of all the factors governing the success of D day, the general felt that one of the most important would be GI morale. Although it took a great deal of his time, he visited airfields, ships, camps, and hospitals to talk to the men who soon would be risking their lives in the invasion. He required his staff to do the same, hoping to instill a feeling of teamwork from the top generals to the lowest privates. At one location, sailors stood at attention in a heavy rain waiting for him to arrive. When Ike came to review them, he removed his raincoat and won their immediate respect and devotion.

Now the stage was set for the greatest amphibious assault in history. It had been planned with painstaking detail by thousands of men. Each individual had his own job of gathering and interpreting data. Then someone else gathered all the information and made certain that each piece became a part of the larger plan. Finally, someone had to assume the responsibility of putting the plan into action. It all came down to General Eisenhower.

On June 2, he moved SHAEF headquarters to an estate north of Portsmouth near the embarkation area. His own personal quarters were located in a trailer near his office/tent. The following day bad news came in the form of a report that a low-pressure weather system was headed for the French coast, bringing with it low clouds, rain, and fierce winds.

As the general and his staff met for dinner that night, wind and rain rattled the windows. Someone reminded Ike that the weather was always neutral in a war, but at that moment he saw it dressed in a German uniform. There was still time to postpone the invasion and he held off until the following morning at the regular four o'clock meeting.

The weather report continued to be dismal. Air support would be hopeless in weather like this; the waves and wind would combine to make landing hazardous. The general postponed the invasion for twenty-four hours.

The next morning, General Eisenhower drove through wind and rain over muddy roads to his waiting staff. Good news waited for him, too, as the meteorologist predicted gradually clearing skies for the next thirty-six hours, followed by more wind and rain.

Eisenhower paced the library as the others watched. Another delay could be demoralizing for the troops, could lead to security leaks and a much longer postponement of the invasion until conditions were just right again.

At 4:15 A.M., Ike made up his mind. He thought for another moment, then said in a decisive voice, "Okay, let's go." The order

June 6, 1944. General Eisenhower visits with paratroopers before they assist in launching the invasion of the continent. Courtesy, Signal Corps

was given for the invasion to begin the next day, June 6, 1944. Now he could do nothing more but wait.

The invasion began as more than eight thousand planes carried out a saturation bombing. Then minesweepers crossed the channel to the five landing beaches, clearing a path for the soldiers. Before daylight, battleships and cruisers laid down a barrage, followed by a demolition team who dynamited beach obstructions.

The landings began by Americans on Utah and Omaha Beaches while Canadians and British landed on Gold, Juno, and Sword Beaches. The news was good enough the next morning to make the general smile, and the news continued to be better than expected throughout the day. Only at Omaha Beach were troops pinned down by heavy enemy fire as wave after wave of Americans failed to reach the shore. Ike ordered a bombardment of

German gun battlements and, by evening, the Omaha sector was safe enough for landings.

When Eisenhower went to bed that night, he could reflect that 156,000 Allied troops invaded Hitler's Europe that day, with only twenty five hundred casualties, primarily at Omaha Beach. It was a good beginning.

On D-day-plus-one, Eisenhower went across the channel in a minelayer, dropping anchor off Omaha Beach. General Bradley, commander of the U.S. First Army, came aboard. He told Ike that the troops had moved off the beaches and were going inland, despite heavy German fighting. Later Eisenhower met with Field Marshal Montgomery to receive similar news. Still later, Ike asked the ship's captain to take him closer to shore so that he could see more.

On June 10, General Marshall arrived in London from the United States with some aides and they wanted to see the battlefields. They went ashore with Ike at Normandy and found that the beaches were secure, the artificial harbors were in place and being used. The only airplanes in evidence belonged to the Allies.

By the end of June, however, the Normandy battle had slowed down. Small fields made it hard for tanks to operate and soldiers had to move from hedgerow to hedgerow to advance.

There was another reason for the slowdown. British Field Marshal Montgomery had promised to take the pivotal city of Caen by this time, but had not done so. His caution and delays drove Ike and his staff to the brink of asking for Monty's resignation.

Seven weeks after the invasion, the beach front was only eighty miles long, the deepest inland penetration about thirty miles. Eisenhower couldn't wait any longer. First, he sent Major General J. Lawton "Lightnin' Joe" Collins and the American Seventh Corps to take the port city of Cherbourg and asked General Bradley to work on a plan to break out of the beach stalemate.

It began on July 25 and, within a few days, Bradley's troops had penetrated German lines. General Patton and his Third Army arrived on the continent and began their march through France on August 1. Two days later they were halfway to Paris.

The French coast was secure in this area when Eisenhower and Marshall went ashore four days after the invasion. Courtesy, U.S. Navy

Eisenhower coached his commanders as if he were coaching a football team, urging them from one play to the next. Bradley and Patton and Collins needed little encouragement. It was Montgomery who needed constant reminders to move his troops. In the midst of this, Eisenhower had to outflank Churchill. The subject was a plan to invade southern France and take the city of Marseilles. Eisenhower recommended an August 15 landing, but Churchill still held out for invading the Balkan countries before the Russians did. Ike reminded Churchill that his own job was to defeat Nazi Germany, not to engage in postwar Balkan politics. Ike's plan proceeded on schedule.

By mid-August all of the Allied armies were converging on Paris. For the honor of liberating the city, Eisenhower chose General Jacques Philippe Lecler and his American-equipped Second French Army. Germans inside the city surrendered on August 25, and de Gaulle entered the city that evening, receiving a hero's welcome. Eisenhower stayed away until August 28, when he rode in a wild, joyous parade given in his honor. On the 30th, de Gaulle announced the forming of a provisional government of France. Roosevelt refused to recognize it because of his distrust of the French leader's capability.

By September, Eisenhower was several weeks ahead of OVER-LORD's schedule, and he moved his headquarters from England to Versailles, just outside of Paris. In the United States, there were great expectations of peace, but Eisenhower knew that Hitler and his troops would fight to the end. He cautioned everyone to go easy on victory talk.

As the Allies rolled through France, Eisenhower announced in October that he was turning over control of the country to de Gaulle, and Roosevelt was forced to recognize that France could no longer be held under military control. The relationship between France and the United States was not a warm one, because of the hostility between the two countries' leaders. But at least a relationship existed, thanks to Eisenhower. He had been thrust between two great egos and forced to swallow his own quick temper as he worked out compromise after compromise. He was learning the art of political maneuverings even as he practiced military ones.

Now that France had been liberated, the Allies could turn full attention to defeating Germany. Eisenhower was besieged by his field commanders, Montgomery, Bradley, and Patton, to listen to their plans to bring this about. Although he listened, Ike's own military philosophy prevailed. Controversy continued to plague Eisenhower's orders until the end of the war as he stood up to arguments from all his generals. That he managed to do so is a measure of his own inner strength. He weighed all the information, considered all possibilities, and then made his decisions. He was the supreme commander and he acted like one.

The Allied commanders knew that heavy fighting still lay ahead. The temptation in late October was to wait until spring when more supplies and good weather would arrive. Although Patton and his

General Eisenhower visits with a GI in Belgium, November, 1944.

army took the German city of Metz on November 23, everywhere else the offensive stopped.

On December 16, Eisenhower learned that he had just been promoted to a five-star general of the army. He now commanded fifty-four divisions on a five-hundred-mile front, with the smallest concentration of troops in the Ardennes Forest region in southeast Belgium.

The shortage of troops in this area was disturbing to Bradley, and he came to Eisenhower's quarters that same day to talk about it. As they talked, a message arrived saying that the Germans had launched a counteroffensive in the Ardennes. Again the weather favored the Germans as heavy fog grounded Allied planes. Without air reconnaissance, the heavy buildup of German infantry and tanks went undiscovered. Soon twenty-four German panzer divisions began to drive hard through Belgium. Their goal was to capture the large supply depots near Liege. The German breakthrough looked like a bulge in Allied lines and reporters quickly dubbed it "the Battle of the Bulge."

Eisenhower called a staff meeting to decide on a course of action. He wanted to bring in armored divisions from the north and south to squeeze the enemy between them. On December 19, Ike wired Montgomery to "plug the holes in the north," and he told Patton to launch an attack from the south.

Now the eyes of the world turned to the small town of Bastogne and the American troops there who were being encircled by a German force several times larger than they. The weather was terrible, supplies short, and the Germans merciless. On December 22, the German commander demanded that the Americans surrender. American Brigadier General Anthony McAuliffe sent back a one-word reply: "Nuts."

Good weather the following day allowed the Allies to send in supplies to the forces at Bastogne and also bomb the Germans. Although snow and ice covered most of the roads in the area, fierce fighting continued into January when the German drive ground to a halt. The Battle of the Bulge had been won by the Allies, but at a great cost in men and morale.

Eisenhower thought ahead to final victory now, devising a campaign in which all his armies would fight their way to the Rhine, encircle the industrial Ruhr Valley, and then fan out and overrun Germany. During this time of preparation, Ike reread a childhood hero, Hannibal, discussing with his aides that military strategist's encirclement of the Romans.

Marshall agreed with Ike's plan, but there were objections from his field commanders, primarily due to individual egos rather than military reasons. But Eisenhower prevailed again, and his plan was implemented.

In early February, the Allies attacked all along the Rhine River, finding stubborn resistance at first. But as German oil reserves were depleted by constant bombing, the resistance diminished. Then they moved across the river after capturing a strategic railroad bridge at Remagen. By April 1, seven Allied armies were across, beginning a division-by-division capture of the German army. Continued fighting seemed pointless to Eisenhower, and he issued a proclamation to German soldiers and civilians to lay down their arms and plant spring crops.

But Hitler was still in charge, issuing wild orders to his remaining soldiers and followers. Ike soon realized that German defeat would come only when the Allies had overrun all of the crumbling nation, so he gave the orders to push eastward to the Elbe River.

Eisenhower gave Bradley's Twelfth Army Group the primary responsibility of capturing as much of the remaining German army as it could. After some thought, Ike decided to leave the capture of Berlin to the Russian army.

This became his most criticized move of the entire war. Critics said that by leaving the Russians to take Berlin, Ike had lost the best opportunity the Allies had to prevent Communist control of eastern Germany and eastern Europe. But nothing would have driven the Russians out of territory already conquered, and they were now only thirty miles from Berlin while the Allies were still three hundred miles away. Besides, the matter already had been decided by Churchill, Stalin, and Roosevelt at the Yalta conference in early February. It was then that they agreed to split the city into three sectors, one governed by each of the major Allied powers. The question of who captured it first would not change that.

As the Allied armies pushed out in all directions, Ike visited troops at the front, watching their accomplishments and sharing a great sense of pride. He wanted Marshall to join him and see for himself what the armies he had helped to create were doing. Ike wrote in mid-April, "I think you should make a visit here while we are still conducting a general offensive." President Roosevelt's death on April 12, however, prevented Marshall from making the trip.

In late April, the Russians fought their way into Berlin at a cost of more than one hundred thousand men. Two months later, they would give control of two-thirds of the city over to the United States and Britain, neither of whom lost even one of their soldiers.

Winston Churchill was a frequent visitor of Eisenhower's during the battle to free Europe. Northern France, March, 1945.

Hitler committed suicide on April 30, and the Nazis soon asked to surrender to Britain and the United States. Eisenhower refused this offer, saying there must be a full and unconditional surrender to all Allies. The Germans begged that three million Germans be allowed to leave Czechoslovakia to avoid capture by the Russians. Eisenhower refused, reminding them of the more than fifteen million Russians killed in battle and the six million Jews starved and gassed in concentration camps.

On the morning of May 7, 1945, the Germans surrendered totally and unconditionally to the Allies at SHAEF forward headquarters at Rheims, France. Everyone agreed to a cease-fire at midnight, May 8.

May 7, 1945, Allied Headquarters, Rheims, France, following the sur-
render of the German Army. Left to right: Lieutenant General Sir
F. E. Morgan, Lieutenant General Walter B. Smith, Captain Harry C.
Butcher, General Eisenhower, Sir Arthur Tedder, Admiral Sir Harold
M. Burrough. An unidentified Russian officer stands to extreme left.

Then Eisenhower broadcast this message to the world:

"Just a few minutes ago Germany surrendered all her remaining
forces on land and sea. They have been thoroughly whipped and
the surrender is unconditional. . . . To every subordinate who has
been in this command of almost five million men I owe a debt of
gratitude that can never be repaid."

Everywhere in the free world, millions of people were feeling
the same way about him.

9

The Peacetime Years

Ike was bone-weary and wanted nothing more than to go home to Mamie now that the war was won. But he was a world hero and everyone wanted to see him, touch him, honor him in some way. As soon as the peace treaty was signed in Rheims, he traveled to London, Brussels, The Hague, and Prague. Victory parades and celebrations were staged in his honor. He received the Cross of Liberation from France and the Order of Merit from Great Britain, the first American ever to receive the latter.

The highlight of the victory celebrations came on June 12, at Guildhall in London. Churchill asked Eisenhower to participate in a formal ceremony, make the principal speech, and then receive the Duke of Wellington's sword.

Eisenhower took his speech seriously, working on it for nearly three weeks. His simple yet eloquent words stand as some of his finest. "I come from the heart of America," he said. Then he spoke of the differences between Americans and British, but of their similarities, too. He spoke of the Allied team and insisted that he was only a symbol and that the awards and acclaim coming his way should go to others. He was a good coach who always remembered his team.

Finally he came home to the United States in mid-June, hoping to go to the thirtieth reunion of his class at West Point. Again he was involved in victory parades in New York and Washington where people waited hours to see him pass by. But his happiest moment came in Kansas when his pacifist mother joined him on a reviewing stand.

While he was in the United States, talk about his candidacy for president came up again. President Truman said he would support him for the presidency in 1948, and friends were eager to start clubs to promote him. But he would have none of it. To Mamie he wrote later, "Many people seem astounded that I'd have no slightest interest in politics."

Ike really wanted to retire with Mamie at his side. Instead, he returned to Europe early in July, 1945, to become commander of the U.S. Occupation Zone governing postwar Germany. Mamie was not allowed to join him in Frankfurt where he lived and worked.

Serious problems remained even with the war over. Soon after Ike returned, he traveled to Berlin where President Truman met with Prime Minister Churchill and Premier Stalin at the Potsdam Conference. The purpose of this conference was to establish territorial settlements between Germany and its neighbors. Eisenhower told Truman that the United States should not agree to dismantling Germany industry. Germany's industrial know-how and natural resources were needed for the recovery of all Europe. Nevertheless, Truman signed the Potsdam Declaration, which called for limitations on German production.

Eisenhower also gave Truman other advice which he ignored. Ike had been briefed about the atomic bomb before he went to the conference and felt depressed when he heard about it. When he found a chance, he suggested to the president that the bomb not be used.

Trips around Europe depressed the general even more. He saw the complete ruin of Germany as well as the horror of concentration camps. When he went to Russia in August, he saw that it had suffered even more than the rest of Europe. This only helped to convince him that the atomic bomb should never be used and that future wars be avoided at all costs.

While Eisenhower was a guest of the Russian government, he was treated like a conquering hero. On August 12, a parade was staged in his honor and he was invited by Stalin to the reviewing stand on top of Lenin's tomb. No foreigner had been given this honor before. Everywhere he went in Russia, he told the people, "Our two countries must learn to understand each other."

He was still in Russia when it was announced that the United States had dropped the atom bomb on two Japanese cities. On August 14, 1945, peace was declared in the Pacific theater of war.

Five months after the war officially ended, Eisenhower came home to the United States to stay, replacing George Marshall as chief of staff. It became a thankless job as he tried to convince Congress that demobilization of the army should not be done. Eisenhower sincerely believed that the postwar army should remain strong to keep the peace.

He also believed that an international system of controlling atomic energy should be established. He hoped that, through the United Nations, atomic energy buildups around the world might be controlled.

The general took on extra duties in 1947 when he became an adviser to the newly created Department of Defense. But he was tired now. "There is nothing I want so much as an opportunity to retire," he wrote to his old friend, Swede Hazlett. It was not until February, 1948, that he could do so, and then only retire from the army at that. There were far too many other things left for him to accomplish to retire completely.

He was fifty-eight years old, had spent thirty-seven of those years in the military, and now had his choice of any career he wanted. There was constant pressure to run for the presidency, but he said no again and again. Many companies wanted him to become their president or representative, and again he said no.

Then he was asked to become president of Columbia University in New York City. He accepted this offer if he could first write his remembrances of World War II. His book, *Crusade in Europe*, became a best-seller when it was published in 1948. It was translated into twenty-two languages, added to his popularity, and made him a wealthy man.

Eisenhower was soon installed as president of Columbia, and most of the trustees were pleased. Many faculty members, how-

June, 1948. General Eisenhower is installed as president of Columbia University, New York City. Seated in first row left to right: Milton Eisenhower, son John, Mamie. Courtesy, Columbia University

1948 or 1949. Always interested in football, Eisenhower attends practice session with Lou Little, Columbia University football coach. Courtesy, Columbia University

ever, were not. He was not a scholar by any means, and he was an ex-military man besides.

Five months later, it sounded as if Ike wasn't too happy there either, telling a friend he was afraid he had made a terrible mistake. His main problem was that he couldn't adjust to the academic life after having been a military man for so long. Other problems stemmed from the demands on his time and the small challenge the job offered. Probably he was simply bored.

On June 25, 1950, Communist North Korea invaded the Republic of South Korea, and President Truman ordered General

MacArthur to take charge of its defense. The U.S. Navy and Air Force were sent to Korea immediately, with ground troops to follow. With the nation again at war and the world thrown into confusion over this Communist aggression, Eisenhower longed to be in the center of things again. He didn't have long to wait.

In October, 1950, Truman asked Eisenhower to take charge of NATO's armed forces in Europe. NATO was the North Atlantic Treaty Organization begun a year earlier by eleven European nations. It was designed for mutual protection in case of attack by an outside nation.

The Eisenhowers had just bought a farm near Gettysburg, Pennsylvania, which appealed to them for many reasons. First, their son, John, had married in 1947, and now had given them two grandchildren, Dwight David II and Barbara Anne. Two more grandchildren would be born in the next several years.

The Eisenhowers were doting grandparents and wanted a place where they could enjoy the children's company, out of the public eye. They also liked the idea of conducting a successful farming business similar to the one established by Ike's grandfather so long ago. Now they would have to turn over the work of building a new house and revitalizing the land to others while they moved to Paris and the general took charge of NATO's defense.

He began this new tour of duty with a trip that took him to all of the eleven European countries in NATO. He tried to unite them in a joint defense effort, with each contributing its specialties. It was difficult, however, to persuade old enemies to work together. France and England were especially distrustful of Germany.

In February, he flew back to the United States to deliver a speech to a joint session of Congress. Here it became his job to convince congressmen that some of the defense forces in NATO should be American soldiers and military supplies.

Eisenhower's job was a difficult one, and he worked long hours convincing European nations that NATO would benefit them. He and Mamie entertained a constant stream of visitors at their rented home outside of Paris. Many were official guests coming to discuss NATO problems. But others were close friends who came to help

April 12, 1951. On duty with NATO, General Eisenhower visits the second Armored Cavalry Division at Augsburg, Germany. Courtesy, Army Signal Corps

him relax. They also came to remind him that they were ready to start his campaign for the presidency whenever he was.

Senator Henry Cabot Lodge of Massachusetts was one person who constantly urged the general to run for president. He pointed out that if Ike didn't, Senator Robert A. Taft would probably get the nomination by the Republican Party. Taft opposed NATO and did not support American participation in European or Asian affairs. He was an isolationist, and Eisenhower did not believe in this philosophy.

Pressure began to mount through the year as more and more people urged him to become a candidate. But he would not enter into the political hassle of fighting over delegates or making speeches. Not yet, anyway. Not until he was convinced that the American voters really wanted him to run for the presidency.

This happened in the New Hampshire primary on March 11, 1952, when Eisenhower beat his principal opponent, Robert A. Taft, with 50 percent of the vote. Ike's name had been entered on the Republican ballot in January by Lodge, who hoped to persuade the general to run. Although Eisenhower was upset when he learned his name had been placed on the ballot without his permission, he did not ask that it be removed.

A week later, Eisenhower received more than one hundred thousand write-in votes in Minnesota. On June 1, he asked President Truman to accept his resignation from NATO and his retirement as general of the army. Then he became a full-time candidate for the presidency.

Ike flew to Abilene for his first campaign speech, which was given in the rain to a half-empty grandstand. It wasn't a good speech nor was it spoken well. The next day, however, Eisenhower gave a press conference and showed everyone once again that he was master of this form of communication. He wasn't afraid to answer questions directly and his sincerity showed. Reporters loved him, even if they didn't always agree with his politics.

Now the fight began for delegates to the Republican National Convention scheduled to open in July in Chicago. Senator Taft already had many, almost enough to win the nomination. But an undercurrent of support had begun for Eisenhower and delegates switched to him. He was nominated on the first ballot. Richard M. Nixon was nominated to run as the vice-presidential candidate.

The Democratic Party chose Governor Adlai E. Stevenson of Illinois as their candidate and, by Labor Day, both presidential nominees and running mates were crisscrossing the country, making speeches and looking for votes.

Eisenhower's schedule wasn't designed for a weak person. At sixty-one, he was much more active, vigorous, and energetic than Stevenson, who was nine years younger. Ike traveled more, spoke more, held more press conferences. In the eight weeks before election day, Eisenhower traveled more than fifty-one thousand miles through forty-five states and gave 232 speeches. The high point came in Detroit in October when he announced that he would "... concentrate on the job of ending the Korean war ..." by making a trip there after the election. With this statement, Eisenhower added to his lead in the prediction polls.

Early on election day, returns put Eisenhower ahead. By evening it was obvious that he had won in a landslide, carrying thirty-nine of the forty-eight states and receiving 55.1 percent of the votes.

At 2:00 A.M. following election day, the Eisenhowers joined the Republican crowd at the Commodore Hotel in New York City. To the celebrating audience Ike said, "This is a time of dedication rather than triumph."

Then Ike and Mamie went out to their car to go home to bed. It was then they discovered that their driver of many years had been replaced by two strangers—Secret Service men. Now Ike knew that he was truly the president-elect.

10

The First

Administration
(GREAT CRUSADE) X

In order to fulfill his campaign promise, President-elect Eisenhower flew to Korea on November 29, 1952. He did what he often did during World War II, he visited the front lines. Dressed in a heavy jacket and fur-lined hat as protection from the bitter cold, he talked to enlisted men and flew reconnaissance missions.

But the trip brought no real results. An offensive could not be carried out because of the strength of the enemy. And peace negotiations, which had been going on for nearly two years, were stalemated.

When Ike's ship docked in Hawaii he told the press: "We face an enemy whom we cannot hope to impress by words, however eloquent, but only by deeds—executed under circumstances of our own choosing."

At home he began to select members of his cabinet. Because he had been involved in politics only briefly and civilian life more briefly still, he had to depend upon friends to recommend candidates. Many of those appointed were business executives. After a leading newspaper remarked that Ike's cabinet consisted of eight millionaires and a plumber, he worried that his administration would be remembered as reflecting only the businessman's point of view.

His first appointment, and perhaps most important, was John Foster Dulles as secretary of state. Dulles was a corporation attorney representing many business firms in international affairs, and he had written the Japanese Peace Treaty while Truman was president. Dulles was perhaps the best qualified man in the coun-

January 20, 1953. President Eisenhower's first inauguration. Four presidents are shown in photograph left to right: Harry Truman, Herbert Hoover, Dwight Eisenhower, Richard Nixon. Courtesy, National Park Service

try to lead its foreign affairs department. Eisenhower's old wartime chief of staff, Walter B. Smith, became undersecretary of state. He was the only personal friend appointed by the president-elect. Now the coach had a new team and was ready to direct the plays.

Inauguration day, January 20, 1953, was sunny but chilly. With outgoing President Truman, Eisenhower walked through the rotunda of the Capitol building to the east front. A platform had been erected there for the ceremonies. The crowd was the largest thus far in American history and came prepared to celebrate. Republicans especially had something to shout about: Ike was their first elected president since 1928.

Wearing a dark blue, double-breasted overcoat over a business suit, Eisenhower took the oath of office. Then he delivered his inaugural address, after first reading a prayer he had written that morning. He spoke of challenges that had to be faced and he promised that his administration would "neither compromise, nor tire, nor ever cease" to seek worldwide peace.

As president, Ike followed a schedule he had established long ago. He arose early, around 6:00 A.M. While eating a small breakfast, he read several newspapers. He read very quickly and when he was pleased about something, he often sent a word of praise to the writer. He was in his office by 8:00 A.M., where he worked until lunchtime. Usually it was a working lunch. Back at his desk, he would continue until 6:00 P.M. The day was one of constant decision-making and unceasing pressure.

If he did not have to put in an appearance at a government meeting or a social function, the president was happy to have dinner quietly with Mamie. Often they ate in front of the television set watching the news. Then he worked until 11:00 P.M. on official reports or proposals. Finally he stopped to enjoy an hour of painting before going to bed at midnight.

Painting was his latest hobby, developed during the war through the encouragement of Winston Churchill. He added it to his other pastimes of fishing and playing golf and bridge. These hobbies gave him an occasional brief release from his ever-increasing responsibilities. He shared his painting time with no one, but he played golf and bridge with a small group of close friends. With them he could be himself.

He was discovering, however, that it was almost impossible to maintain the same kind of friendships that he had enjoyed before becoming president. When General Bradley, a friend since West Point days, telephoned, he addressed him as "Mr. President." It was correct procedure, but a far cry from the days when everyone simply called him Ike.

In February, Eisenhower held his first press conference. As he had done during and after the war, he made friends with reporters due to his open, direct, and friendly manner. Often he praised them for the sympathetic treatment he received at their hands. Occasionally, however, he was mystified that a reporter could be a friend of his and still criticize his policies.

One of the first policies that came under harsh criticism was his handling of the Senator Joseph McCarthy problem. For two years, McCarthy, the Republican Senator from Wisconsin, had been hammering at the theme of disloyalty in American life. He had convinced many people that Communists had infiltrated the government and its agencies. Now he was trying to oust them.

With a Republican president in the White House and a Republican majority in Congress, McCarthy's power became even stronger as he continued to attack government agencies and employees. Eisenhower was being pressured on all sides to take action against McCarthy. But the president did not want to become involved in a verbal battle with the senator. He felt it was undignified for the office of the presidency to deal with a problem that could become a personality conflict. Rather, he looked to the Senate to reduce McCarthy's power legally.

McCarthy's investigations ran unchecked for nearly two more years, although the president stepped in from time to time to deplore his antics and criticize his methods. Finally in April, 1954, a series of Senate hearings were televised. These hearings fully exposed McCarthy's shoddy tactics and irresponsible methods to the American public, and in December the Senate voted to censure the senator, reducing his power and influence in the country. The president's policy toward McCarthy was finally vindicated.

President Eisenhower dealt with many issues during his first years in office. These included taxes, the budget, the war in Korea, the level of defense spending, foreign aid, and the problem of world peace.

Defense spending was something familiar to him. As a military officer, he had testified before many congressional committees. As president, he now advocated large cutbacks in the defense budget over the objections of many politicians.

One of the best ways to reduce defense spending, he thought, was to pursue peace. Since World War II ended in 1945, the

United States and the Soviet Union had been hurling insults so fierce it sounded as if they wouldn't stop until they were hurling atom bombs.

Then, with Eisenhower's election, and Stalin's death following a few months later in March, 1953, it seemed that a fresh start might be possible.

The president believed this sincerely, saying to one of his assistants soon after, "The slate is clean. Now let us begin talking to each other." He then instructed his writers to work on a speech about peace. Many of the words were his own, as he oversaw every draft, contributing many sentences and phrases. Called "The Chance for Peace," the speech is thought to be one of the finest of his presidency.

"The world in arms is not spending money alone," he said. "It is spending the sweat of its laborers, the genius of its scientists, the hopes of its children." He concluded by saying that a percentage of the savings from disarmament could be contributed to a fund for world aid and reconstruction. This fund would "assist all peoples to know the blessings of productive freedom."

In July, 1953, an armistice was signed in Korea, ending the war there. It was a compromise settlement at best, but Eisenhower was pleased with it. The man of war in the forties had become the peacemaker of the fifties.

In December Eisenhower gave his "Atoms for Peace" speech to the General Assembly of the United Nations. He discussed in detail the destructive elements of atomic warfare and the arms race underway. He suggested that an International Atomic Energy Agency be organized under the sponsorship of the United Nations to study ways to use atomic energy for peaceful activities. It would "serve the needs rather than the fears of mankind," he stated.

The thirty-five hundred U.N. delegates cheered him and worldwide reaction to the speech was positive. But the Russians didn't respond. It wasn't until 1957 that the International Atomic Energy Agency was created. By then the arms race had moved to new levels and the world's knowledge of atomic power had grown beyond the concept and capabilities of the Agency. The Russians could not, or would not, cooperate with the president's "Atoms for Peace" plan and it was abandoned.

Eisenhower considered it a rejection of one of the major goals of his presidency.

Although peace had been achieved in Korea, small skirmishes and battles continued to break out elsewhere. French Indochina's three states of Cambodia, Laos, and Vietnam were special trouble spots. For seven years, the French had been fighting a losing battle against the Communists there. Now the French were tired, worn out. Eisenhower was urged by many advisers and Congress to intervene in order to halt the spread of Communism.

The president weighed matters carefully and decided against intervention. Instead he suggested that France grant independence to the three states, hoping to defuse the fighting. The French refused and, after a bloody battle at Dien Bien Phu, Laos and Cambodia were given full independence anyway, and Vietnam was split into two states.

Through these actions in his first two years as president, Eisenhower's supporters would be able to say that he had gotten the country out of Korea and kept it out of Vietnam.

Eisenhower then organized the Southeast Asia Treaty Organization (SEATO), which was a form of NATO. In it, the United States pledged its aid for mutual defense in Southeast Asia in case of Communist attack.

Fighting continued to break out in the Far East. When the Chinese Communists bombarded the small island of Quemoy, an island near territory held by Nationalist China, it was thought that another world war might begin. Eisenhower was urged to consider counterattacks including using the atomic bomb.

But Eisenhower did what he did best. He considered all sides of the problem, asked for advice from experts, and finally followed his own ideas. He deliberately kept the Communists guessing until they decided not to attack. No one knew whether he planned to use atomic weapons. And the Communists could not risk the chance that he might. Once again, he kept the peace.

Domestic matters needed the president's attention as well. Many

President Eisenhower signs the St. Lawrence Seaway Bill, May 13, 1954.

bills sent to Congress under his guidance were approved. One was to create the St. Lawrence Seaway, which finally won approval after a twenty-five-year fight. Congress, however turned down Ike's bill supporting voting rights for eighteen-year-olds.

A short recession occurred in 1954, but ended soon, thanks in part to extension of Social Security and unemployment benefits and the raising of the minimum wage to a dollar an hour. Lowering taxes also helped. These were bills or acts supported by the president. A buying spree was soon underway in the United States and, for the first time, many citizens could afford to buy automobiles.

But where to drive them? That was the question bothering the president. He had been concerned for many years about the poor interstate highway system in the United States. Now, in early 1955, he decided to do something about it and pushed for a highway program to be funded by bond issues and special taxes. Congress, however, failed to pass it until nearly two years later when the National System of Interstate and Defense Highways Bill was

DULLES   CHURCHILL   EISENHOWER

enacted. It became Eisenhower's favorite piece of legislation passed during his presidency.

In the spring of 1955, it appeared that friendlier relations with the Soviet Union might be possible. Nikita Khrushchev was the new Russian leader and he seemed eager to show that he was a peaceful man. Anthony Eden, the new Prime Minister of England, called for an East-West conference to be held in Switzerland. In July, leaders of the United States, Russia, Great Britain, and France met for a week of talks during which Eisenhower proposed his Open Skies plan. This plan gave Soviets and Americans an opportunity to look at one another's military bases and even photograph them if they wished.

June 25, 1954. Sir Winston Churchill and Sir Anthony Eden meet at the White House with President Eisenhower and John Foster Dulles.

THE COLD WAR
MAR. 12, 1947
DEC. 8, 1987

EDEN

France and Great Britain approved, but Khrushchev said no, that it was an espionage plot against the Soviet Union. The conference ended without much being accomplished. But it was a dramatic moment in diplomatic struggles during the period called the Cold War.

In late August, President and Mrs. Eisenhower flew to Colorado for a month's vacation. He was tired and strained from his duties and looked forward to fishing, a few games of bridge, and some golf with friends. An office was provided him at Lowry Air Force Base where he could work a few hours each day when needed.

On September 23, while playing golf, the president stopped to eat lunch with a friend. He ate a hamburger smothered with

President and Mrs. Eisenhower during the 1956 campaign for reelection,
Washington, D.C.

onions. As he continued playing, he felt what he thought was an attack of indigestion and finally went home to his mother-in-law's where he and Mamie were staying.

That night he was awakened by sharp pains in his chest. Mamie called the doctor, who realized the president was having a heart attack. Early the next morning he was admitted to the hospital, where he remained for seven weeks. During his time there, as he grew better, he could sit in a chair and sign papers that only the president could sign.

In mid-November, Ike was well enough to fly back to Washington and then to Gettysburg, where he would stay until his health was fully restored.

With the arrival of 1956, Congress, the press, and citizens began to wonder if the president would seek a second term. They didn't have to wait long to find out. On February 29, he said at a press conference, "I have reached a decision. My answer will be positive." He had decided to run for a second term.

Although fully recovered from his heart attack, the president soon became ill again. In June, he underwent a serious operation for an intestinal blockage. Several weeks later he flew to Panama to attend a meeting of the Organization of American States. He went because of his vital interest in the organization, but he also may have gone to show that he was fully recovered from his surgery.

Heads of state met for three days and then Eisenhower returned. He seemed to have regained his strength completely, and there was no doubt now that he was ready to run for reelection and would welcome a second term.

11

The Second Administration

The Democrats nominated Adlai Stevenson for president once again and he began to campaign on two issues: reducing the military draft and suspending nuclear testing.

President Eisenhower was renominated by the Republicans at their convention held in San Francisco during August. Everyone wore "I like Ike" buttons, and victory was already in the air. Politicians reminded everyone that the president had given the country four years of peace and prosperity. It would be foolish not to reelect him for four more years of the same. And voters seemed to agree. Polls showed Eisenhower's popularity even greater than in 1952.

Meanwhile Ike couldn't relax for a moment to enjoy his popularity. There were always problems. Even as he was being nominated a second time, a situation in the Middle East was threatening to blow up into another world war if something wasn't done soon. Once again, Eisenhower was placed in the role of peacemaker.

The trouble spot was Egypt, where Gamal Abdel Nasser had taken over the government in 1954. Nasser knew that both the Communist world and the Western powers wanted an ally in the Middle East. He used this knowledge by playing one side against the other. To gain favor with Egypt, Russia sent tanks and planes while the West promised help in building the Aswan Dam on the Nile River.

Nasser began to irritate the Western powers by his actions, however, and finally the United States and Britain withdrew the offer to help build the dam. On July 26, an angry Nasser took

100

control of the Suez Canal from the British, who controlled it by treaty. Nasser said he would use the profits from running it to build the Aswan Dam himself.

The British and French considered this act a threat to the security of navigation in the canal. Soon reports surfaced that they would take military action to recover the Canal Zone. Eisenhower felt that his old allies would make a mistake if they attacked, saying that "Nasser was within his rights." He suggested a conference between the involved nations, hoping to hold off military actions.

Conferences were held by committees and individuals, with Secretary of State Dulles flying from one capital to another to offer suggestions. He proposed larger oil tankers, oil pipe lines going across Turkey and Israel, and even international control of the canal.

Finally Great Britain and France could wait no longer and, with Israel, they attacked Egypt on October 28. There was no doubt that Eisenhower was surprised. He realized that they had been plotting this act of aggression for some time, probably thinking that once it began, the United States would come in on their side. Now the president was going to come up with a surprise of his own.

Eisenhower had some tough decisions to make, but he'd made them before. Basically, he felt the combined action of the three countries could not be allowed to succeed because it was a violation of the Tripartite Declaration. This was an agreement signed by France, Great Britain, and the United States in 1950, vowing to support the victim of an aggression in the Middle East. Now, in 1956, two of the countries that had signed were violating the agreement. Eisenhower felt duty-bound to honor the pledge of this country.

He felt the only way to handle the delicate situation in the Middle East was through the United Nations. After careful consideration, he instructed Dulles to address the General Assembly, asking for adoption of a cease-fire resolution. He asked Dulles to "avoid condemning any nation, but to put his stress on the need for a quick cease-fire."

While the General Assembly was debating the issue, Eisenhower made his last campaign speech in Philadelphia. Naturally he spoke of the Middle East situation. He said, "We cannot subscribe to one law for the weak, another law for the strong; one law for those opposing us, another for those allied with us. There can be only one law—or there will be no peace."

On election day, shortly after noon, Eisenhower heard from Anthony Eden, the Prime Minister of Great Britain, who stated that the British were now willing to accept a cease-fire. The three invading countries agreed to leave the Suez Canal and the Gaza Strip. That evening, Eisenhower, the peacemaker, could settle back and become Eisenhower, the candidate for president. He won by a larger margin than in 1952, although he failed to get a Republican Congress.

The crisis in Egypt was not the only international problem to claim his attention during this time. A serious conflict also began between Hungary and the Soviet Union.

Since the end of World War II, countries bordering Russia had been forced to accept local Communist governments taking orders directly from Moscow. Individual rights had been outlawed so successfully that the Russians believed their neighboring countries would cause no trouble.

They were wrong. Uprisings occurred in many countries, including East Germany, Poland, and now Hungary. Anti-Russian feelings had been especially strong here as free and secret elections showed an overwhelming vote against the Communist government.

In the fall of 1956, persecution of religious and intellectual Hungarian leaders began. On the morning of October 23, students took to the streets of Budapest in protest, beginning an uprising that soon spread across the country. On November 1, the Russians surrounded the capital city and took over airports, sealing the rebelling citizens inside. The Hungarian government appealed to the United States and the United Nations to come to its aid, but President Eisenhower knew the Russians were willing to risk atomic confrontation here. He could do little more than organize an escape route for Hungarian refugees.

Election night, November 6, 1956.

On November 26, Eisenhower welcomed the first refugees to the United States, while agonizing over the thousands who had died in Hungary. The brief revolution was over, but it was a reminder of the threat to individual freedom posed by the Soviet Union.

Many people thought that Eisenhower's second term would be a quiet one. His strong victory at the polls suggested that he would not have to work hard at winning over the public for the programs he wanted. After all, the majority was already on his side. And he had suffered two major illnesses. He would not have the strength, people thought, to conduct a vigorous second term.

Those who thought that way were incorrect. On January 10, 1957, Eisenhower gave his State of the Union address, asking Congress to pass a strong civil rights bill. He wanted to insure fairer treatment of all citizens, especially on the right to vote. When he learned that out of nine hundred thousand blacks in Mississippi, only seven thousand were allowed to vote, he was incensed.

Ike now asked his attorney general to write a civil rights bill. When it was presented to Congress, fights erupted over certain provisions, taking up most of the spring and summer. One particular provision caused the most arguments. It was the part which could find local officials in contempt of court by a federal court if they tried to prevent anyone from registering or voting.

Senators from southern states weakened this amendment by rewriting it to require a jury trial in any contempt action. As jury lists were made from voting lists, which were nearly all white in the South, it seemed unlikely to many that a white jury would convict a white person of violating the rights of a black.

The debate continued into July and the president wrote Swede Hazlett about it. He had corresponded with his old friend from Abilene since they left to go to West Point and the Naval Academy, and he now wrote, "Laws are rarely effective unless they represent the will of the majority."

He went on to say, "There must be . . . respect for the Supreme Court's interpretation of the Constitution—or we shall have chaos.

We cannot possibly imagine a successful form of government in which every individual citizen would have the right to interpret the Constitution according to his own convictions, beliefs, and prejudices."

In a press conference the president was asked if he was aware that he had the power to use military force, if necessary, to put through integration. Ike said that he was aware of it. Then he added, "I can't imagine any set of circumstances that would ever induce me to send federal troops into . . . any area to enforce the orders of a federal court, because I believe that [the] common sense of America will never require it."

This was an agonizing period in Eisenhower's life and it wasn't going to get better, at least for awhile.

The bill, with the trial-by-jury amendment, was passed in late August and criticism from black leaders arose at once. Baseball player Jackie Robinson stated his opposition. So did Philip Randolph, who said, "It is worse than no bill at all." But Martin Luther King, Jr., said that half a loaf was better than no loaf, and he would soon "touch off a massive Negro registration drive."

When this weak form of the Civil Rights Bill reached the president's desk for signature in September, he couldn't decide if he even wanted to sign it. However, it really didn't matter. Events were coming to a showdown in Little Rock, Arkansas, completely overshadowing the bill, which Eisenhower finally signed.

Early in September, Arkansas Governor Orval Faubus called out the National Guard in Little Rock to bar nine black pupils from entering Central High School. A federal judge set a hearing for September 20 to decide the legality of Faubus's action.

Before then, on September 14, the president and the governor met to discuss the situation. Eisenhower suggested to Faubus that he simply change the Guard's orders; that is, to maintain the peace while admitting the black pupils. Faubus seemed to agree.

When Faubus returned to Little Rock, however, he did not withdraw the National Guard, nor did he change their orders. He continued to defy the orders of a federal court. At the hearing on September 20, the federal judge ordered Faubus not to interfere with the progress of integration any longer. A couple of days later, Faubus withdrew the National Guard around the high school.

The president was pleased and that weekend he put on his apron and chef's hat to cook steaks for his friends. Later, while playing bridge, he recalled other crisis situations with which he had dealt. He told his friends that it would be pleasant "to have a short period where things are running smoothly."

The following morning, a racist mob surrounded Central High School in Little Rock, attempting to block the entrance of the nine black students. Three hours later, the students were removed for their own protection.

The president was informed of the situation and hoped that, through calm and deliberate negotiations, the situation would be controlled. But a telegram from the mayor of Little Rock changed his mind: "Situation is out of control and police cannot disperse the mob . . . ," the telegram read.

The president had run out of options, except one. Now he had to use force. A few hours later he ordered troops of the 101st Airborne Division to Little Rock to patrol the school and restore order. "Mob rule cannot be allowed to override the decisions of the courts," he said.

The incident cost the president some popularity with people in the North as well as in the South. But he had taken an oath of office and had no choice but to live up to it. The Little Rock incident continued to make news until it was bumped off the front pages by another crisis called *Sputnik*.

On October 4, 1957, the Russians announced the successful orbiting of *Sputnik*, the first satellite to go beyond the earth's atmosphere. *Sputnik* weighed a little less than two hundred pounds and traveled at a speed of eighteen thousand miles per hour. The Space Age had arrived. X

Since the end of World War II in 1945, Americans thought their country was the richest and most powerful in the world. They also thought they were the best-educated and, in fact, the best in everything. A time of pleasant self-confidence had devel-

X THE SPACE AGE
OCT. 4, 1957
AUG. 31 2011

oped and Americans felt they didn't have much to worry about, especially with a man like Eisenhower in the White House.

Sputnik changed that. The country lost its sense of well-being overnight—changed from a nation of self-confident citizens to one of self-doubters. People were ready to blame someone and, as the president was the most obvious, he became the target, along with members of his administration.

The president hoped to keep the subject out of politics. At a specially called meeting of congressional leaders, he warned Republicans and Democrats alike that neither party could be held liable. He then called a meeting of officials in the Defense Department to find out how the Russians had won the race to space and what the United States could do to advance its own program.

The president then formed a Scientific Advisory Committee to study the problem. But reports from the scientists differed, and Ike found it difficult to make decisions based on conflicting advice.

All areas of government were sending out contradictory signals now. It was a recession year and the president hoped to keep costs down and balance the budget. Yet *Sputnik* had brought demands for increased spending on space research, on Federal aid to colleges and universities, and on fallout shelters for every individual in the country as well as other specialized and expensive projects.

The president was upset by the country's lack of self-confidence showing in government, the press, and the average citizen. He tried to tell everyone, "We face not a temporary emergency . . . but a long-term responsibility."

The launching of the *Sputnik II* on November 3 fueled the situation. A study called the Gaither Report added to the problem by asking the president "to do something." Still he didn't give in to the panic or the pressure, though his calm, thoughtful leadership at the time of *Sputnik* was not fully appreciated by many who had voted for him.

In late November, Ike underwent a routine physical and the results were excellent. A few days later, on November 25, he had a stroke. Until he recovered, Eisenhower allowed Vice President

Richard Nixon to sit in at social and official functions such as dinners and cabinet meetings. But the president was soon back at his desk, though he seemed to be easily upset and more short-tempered than at other times.

Early in 1958, the country experienced another recession, probably its worst since the end of World War II. It had a strong effect on the government's budget, producing a deficit higher than the country had ever known.

While the president struggled with the country's financial condition, he also assumed added duties in foreign affairs. Usually they were handled by his old friend, John Foster Dulles, but now the secretary of state was seriously ill.

Once again, problems were building in the Middle East as Gamal Abdel Nasser tried to unite all the Arab countries. Some countries were agreeable, others were not. Lebanon was one of the latter and, in July, asked for help from the United States.

The president used the Eisenhower Doctrine, a plan passed by Congress, to send American troops to any Middle East nation requesting aid. On the morning of July 14, American forces went ashore at Lebanon to help maintain order in that country.

Chinese Communists began to bombard islands off the shore of Mainland China while, in Latin America, Vice President and Mrs. Nixon were harassed and stoned by organized groups said to be Communist. And on the last day of the year, Fidel Castro and his Communist forces took control of Cuba.

Eisenhower decided he must try to achieve peaceful coexistence with the Communist world. First he sent the vice president to Moscow for a series of meetings with Khrushchev. He then invited the Russian premier to visit the United States.

Khrushchev arrived in September and visited farms in Iowa, held press conferences, argued with American labor leaders, and traveled to Los Angeles. Then he demanded to visit Disneyland, but was not permitted to because the Secret Service felt it could not offer him protection there.

The premier returned to Washington and met the president in a series of talks before returning to Russia. After Khrushchev left,

September 25, 1959. With Nikita Khrushchev during their talks at Camp David, Maryland. Courtesy, U.S. Navy

December 3, 1959. President Eisenhower speaks to the American public
about his coming goodwill tour.
Courtesy, National Park Service

Eisenhower felt the efforts to achieve peace must be continued. In early December he traveled to eleven countries covering three continents, speaking to heads of state about his quest. Everywhere he went, the president was greeted warmly as he pushed for a series of summit meetings to be held the following spring in Paris.

Khrushchev announced in early 1960 that he would attend and then invited President Eisenhower to visit Russia. The premier said that, in honor of the president's visit, the first golf course in Russia would be built.

Eisenhower traveled to South America in February to continue his goodwill tours for peace. Everywhere he went he was greeted warmly. When he returned to Washington, he began to plan for the summit meeting, the Republican convention, and his retirement. In a little more than six months, he would be a private citizen.

On May 1, the president's quest for peace was seriously hurt when a U-2 plane was shot down over Russia. U-2 planes had been flying over the Soviet Union for four years, taking aerial photographs. They were also capable of testing for nuclear activity. These overflights by U-2 planes were no secret to the Russians.

They were no secret to any of the other governments involved with them. The only people who didn't know about U-2 planes were Americans and their representatives in Congress.

At first the U.S. State Department denied that an American plane had been ordered to fly over Russian territory. Later it admitted that what the Russians said was true and that the president knew about it. This angered Khrushchev and he went to the Paris summit meetings ready to destroy them.

When President Eisenhower arrived in Paris for the peace conference, he found that Khrushchev was unwilling to talk with him. Khrushchev continued to be insulting to the president and cancelled his invitation to Russia that summer. The summit was over before it started and Eisenhower packed to return home, depressed and disheartened.

It was a sad time for the world. The leaders of the two most powerful countries had erred as they reached the point of taking serious steps to ban nuclear testing and promote world peace.

The president decided to use the time he would have spent in Russia on another trip, this to the Philippines, Korea, and Formosa. He was asked not to go to Japan because of rioting there, protesting his visit. One million people came out to see him in the Philippines, but his cancelled trip to Japan came as another bitter disappointment.

He returned home and, shortly after, Vice President Richard Nixon was nominated by the Republicans to run for president. Nixon did not immediately ask Eisenhower to campaign for him against the Democratic nominee, John F. Kennedy. Not until October did the president make a number of campaign speeches for Nixon. But it was too late for Nixon. On November 8, 1960, John F. Kennedy was elected by a small margin of votes.

The president was upset over the outcome of the election, and the last ten weeks of his administration were a period of marking time. As a caretaker president, he could do little more than keep the wheels of government running on a smooth course while offering the incoming president advice and assistance.

In December, the president decided to give a farewell address to the country and asked the help of writer Malcolm Moos to research it. Together they wrote one of the president's most memorable speeches in which Ike voiced some of his deepest feelings and greatest fears. Some of the sentences in this speech are the most often quoted and best remembered of his entire career. "In the councils of government," he warned, "we must guard against the acquisition of unwarranted influence . . . by the military-industrial complex." He also directed another warning. "We must avoid . . . plundering the precious resources of tomorrow. . . . We want democracy to survive for all generations to come."

The speech was well received, and the president was in a good mood as inauguration day arrived. On the morning of January 20, he and Mrs. Eisenhower said good-bye to the people in the White House who had served them so well. Then, at noon, Chief Justice Earl Warren administered the oath of office to John F. Kennedy. While all the attention was directed at the Kennedys now, the ex-president and his wife left by a side exit, headed for a private luncheon given by friends and relatives. A little while later, Mr. and Mrs. Eisenhower drove home to Gettysburg, private citizens at last. The presidential years were over. The retirement years had finally begun.

12

The Retirement Years

The president had long thought about retirement. During World War II when he wrote to Mamie, his letters spoke longingly on that subject. He wanted a place to fish, where he could also play golf and bridge, and enjoy his grandchildren. The farm at Gettysburg seemed the ideal place.

The Eisenhowers owned 246 acres and leased 305 more. After buying the farm, they began to raise Angus cattle and hay for the cattle to eat. They also grew other grains, rotating crops to restore the soil to a fertility equal to the days when Ike's ancestors farmed in the area.

The farm was near the Civil War battlefield, and General of the Army Eisenhower (his rank fully restored by President Kennedy) enjoyed visiting the area where the North and the South fought one of their great battles. With old army friends, General Ike played endless games of what-if. What if General Lee had charged here? What if General Meade had attacked here? Even his old ally, British General Montgomery, had comments to make when he visited the Gettysburg battlefield.

During the presidential years, the house had been gutted and rebuilt. Then Mamie decorated it with many of the belongings and mementos they'd accumulated throughout their marriage. Now, finally, the Eisenhowers had a place of their own, rural enough to satisfy them, yet close enough to New York and Washington so friends could come to visit on weekends.

John and his family lived about a mile away, and he became a special assistant to his father. He organized an office for the ex-

The president, pictured earlier on a fishing trip in Rhode Island, September 19, 1958.

President and Mrs. Eisenhower enjoy their Gettysburg farm on an earlier visit, September, 1956.

president on the Gettysburg College campus, and soon the writing of his memoirs began. Eisenhower had written every word of his best-seller, *Crusade in Europe*; now he worked from rough drafts of material given to him by John and several other writers. But much of it was his own work as he revised, rearranged, and wrote additional material.

It was a two-volume work which took four years to write. The first book was called *Mandate for Change*, and the second *Waging Peace*. In these books, Eisenhower tried to analyze his eight years in the White House, but he was reluctant to speak of certain issues such as the McCarthy problem. Nevertheless, his publisher insisted, and he had to do it. Other issues were equally sensitive with the ex-president, especially the U-2 affair. The publisher wanted him to "bare his soul and admit to more mistakes." But Eisenhower would not do it.

When the books were completed, they showed that former President Eisenhower's greatest success was as a peacekeeper, at home and in foreign affairs. He had made peace and kept the peace during his entire administration despite numerous recommendations that the country enter a war to solve a crisis.

First, he had held down the arms race, defying certain senators, the Joint Chiefs of Staff, and the military-industrial complex. In the field of foreign affairs, he had shown his skill in crisis management. During Korea in 1953, Dien Bien Phu in 1954, Quemoy and Matsu in 1955, the Hungarian and Suez crises in 1956, the U-2 crisis in 1960, and others, he had repeatedly kept a cool head. Rather than overreacting, he had conferred, analyzed, and managed each crisis.

In retirement, Eisenhower, as former head of the Republican Party, was asked to speak at fund-raisers, lend his name to causes and appear at more social functions than he could physically manage. According to public polls, Dwight Eisenhower was the most respected and admired man in the country.

In the fall of 1963 conditions in South Vietnam broke down, and President Kennedy committed American troops. This concerned Eisenhower and he followed the situation closely. Kennedy occasionally asked the former president for advice and he gave it freely, if somewhat belligerently at times.

Eisenhower was in New York attending a luncheon at the United Nations when he heard of President Kennedy's assassination on November 22, 1963. The next day, he went to Washington to pay his respects, then called on President Lyndon B. Johnson to offer his support. The two men had differed often during the days when Eisenhower was president and Johnson a senator. They continued to do so now. Nevertheless, Johnson went out of his way to show the ex-president that he was well regarded by the new administration and would welcome his active support and advice.

The presidential election in 1964 kept Johnson and Eisenhower at arm's length for a while, as Johnson became the Democratic candidate and Barry Goldwater, a senator from Arizona, became the Republican's choice. He was not Eisenhower's choice, however. Goldwater's politics were too conservative for Eisenhower's middle-of-the-road approach, although he finally said he would do his best to support Goldwater. In November, Johnson won by a landslide.

Once the election was over and the war in Vietnam had escalated, Johnson called on Eisenhower more and more. Now it was the general's advice he wanted, not the ex-president's. In February, 1965, Eisenhower met for two and one-half hours with Johnson and a group of advisers on how best to wage the war in which they found themselves.

Eisenhower's advice through August of that year remained hawkish, telling Johnson to go for victory. Soon it would change as he found it more and more difficult to approve Johnson's actions.

In November, 1965, the Eisenhowers went to Augusta, Georgia, for a week's holiday, where Ike remarked to Mamie that it had been ten years since his heart attack. The next day he experienced a second heart attack. He was taken to Walter Reed Hospital where he recovered slowly. He was now seventy-five years old.

The former president began to make certain arrangements for his death and decided that he wanted to be buried in Abilene in the Meditation Chapel across the street from his childhood home and west of the Eisenhower Library and Museum. In 1967, Little Icky's body was removed from a Denver cemetery and placed near the spot reserved for the ex-president and Mamie.

Eisenhower continued to keep a busy schedule in Gettysburg and in California, where they spent many winters. Nevertheless, he was slowing down, preferring to reminisce about his early days at Abilene or West Point rather than World War II or the presidency.

In April, 1968, he suffered his third heart attack and was taken to Walter Reed Hospital once again, but he was well enough by summer to become interested in the presidential campaign. Johnson had declared he would not run again, and it seemed certain the Republicans would nominate Nixon. When the Republican convention opened in Miami on August 5, the delegates heard former President Eisenhower endorse Richard Nixon via a message televised from the hospital. The next morning Eisenhower endured another heart attack.

The Place of Meditation, the final resting place of President Eisenhower.

Nixon's victory in November was not by the majority that Eisenhower had hoped, but at least the Republicans had won. The new president asked the old one if he would receive each cabinet appointee, and Eisenhower agreed, replying that he was eager to meet the ones he didn't know.

On November 29, the day of the traditional Army-Navy game, Eisenhower sent a telegram to the Army football coach at West Point. "For 364 days out of the year it is Army, Navy, Air Force, forever. Today it is Army, Army, Army. My heart, though somewhat damaged, will be riding with you and the team. Good luck!" He was still Ike, the football player and coach.

In December, the former president watched the wedding of

President Eisenhower and his grandchildren, Barbara Ann and David, view the inaugural parade with Vice President Nixon and his children, Julie and Tricia, January 21, 1957. David and Julie were married twelve years later.

David Eisenhower, his grandson, to Julie Nixon, the president's daughter, on closed-circuit television. He complained about the length of David's hair but otherwise seemed to enjoy the wedding.

Another operation in early 1969 weakened him further and, in late March, his heart began to fail. The man of action, of decision, and of strength lay still and quiet in his hospital bed, his ruddy face now ghostly pale. But he was ever in command. On March 29, 1969, he gave his last order when he told the doctors to lift him to a sitting position and to lower the shades. Then the room became dark and quiet, and the world waited as his tired old heart finally stopped beating.

Bibliography

Ambrose, Stephen E. *Eisenhower*, Volume I. New York: Simon and Schuster, 1983.

——. *Eisenhower*, Volume II. New York: Simon and Schuster, 1984.

——. *Ike: Abilene to Berlin*. New York: Harper and Row, 1973.

Archer, Jules. *Battlefield President*, Dwight D. Eisenhower. New York: Julian Messner, 1967.

Childs, Marquis. *Eisenhower: Captive Hero*. New York: Harcourt, Brace, Jovanovich, 1958.

Eisenhower, Dwight D. *At Ease: Stories I Tell to Friends*. Garden City, N. Y.: Doubleday & Co., 1967.

——. *Letters to Mamie*. ed. John S. D. Eisenhower. Garden City, N.Y.: Doubleday & Co., 1978.

Eisenhower, John S. D. *Strictly Personal*. Garden City, N. Y.: Doubleday & Co., 1974.

Lyon, Peter. *Eisenhower: Portrait of the Hero*. Boston: Little, Brown and Co., 1974.

Pinkley, Virgil. *Eisenhower, Declassified*. Old Tappan, N. J.: Fleming H. Revell, 1979.

Steinberg, Alfred. *Dwight David Eisenhower*. New York: G.P. Putnam's Sons, 1967.

Index

PRESIDENTS & ADMINISTRATION
NICKNAMES

1. FEDERALIST
2. NEW WASHINGTON
3. REPUBLICAN
4. NATIONAL RIGHTS
5. NATIONAL SURCURITY
6. AMERICAN SYSTEM
7. SPOILS SYSTEM
8. DEMOCRATIC SYSTEM
9. WHIG DOCTINE
10. NO PARTY
11. MANIFEST DESTINY
12. ROUGHT & READY
13. COMPROMISE
14. PRO-SLAVERY
15. SACRED BALANCE
16. EMANCIPATION
17. CONCILLIATION
18. RECONTRUCTION
19. CIVIL REFORM
20. PATRONAGE
21. CIVIL SERVICE
22. SOUND BUSINESS
23. HIGH TARIFF

24. SOUND MONEY
25. OPEN DOOR
26. SQUARE DEAL
27. DOLLAR DIPLOMACY
28. NEW FREEDOM
29. NORMALCY
30. PROHIBITION
31. NEW DAY
32. NEW DEAL
33. FAIR DEAL
34. GREAT CRUSADE
35. NEW FRONTIER
36. GREAT SOCIOTY
37. SILENT MAJORITY
38. W.I.N.
39. NEW SPIRIT
40. FEDERALIST REAGANOMICS
41. NEW BREEZE
42. NEW PROMISE
43. REAL PLANS
44. REAL CHANGE
45.
46.
47.

123